Selling your crap
Online

Selling your crap Online

Caleb Lnenicka

authorHOUSE®

AuthorHouse™
1663 Liberty Drive
Bloomington, IN 47403
www.authorhouse.com
Phone: 1-800-839-8640

Published by AuthorHouse   08/24/2012

ISBN: 978-1-4772-5690-9 (sc)
ISBN: 978-1-4772-5689-3 (e)

Library of Congress Control Number: 2012914413

TABLE OF CONTENTS

ACKNOWLEDGEMENTS

This book is dedicated to my 4 daughters.

First and foremost, I would like to thank my wife for not divorcing me after I sold all of her stuff on Craigslist. Without her support, I would never have been able to achieve my 3 week-old dream of writing a book. Thanks to Dave Berry for taking the amazing picture for the front cover of this book. I didn't think it was possible to make something so beautiful look even more gorgeous. Somehow you did it, though. I would also like to thank everyone who bought things from me on Craigslist. Without you, this book would not have happened. Additional thanks goes to Julie, Johna, Carl (He paid me $1 to have his name in the top 3), Mom & Dad, Noose, Ronnie, Adisa, Rian, Lisa, Obie, Beth, Josh, Ellen, Levi, Jess, Kim, Lindy, Isaac, Carrie, Kelly, Chris, Anne, Melissa, Graham, Matt (all 4 Matt's), Pete, Oliver, Shankle, Matt Damon, James, Larissa, Charlie the Predator, Johnson (even though we've had our differences), Rodney, Kalleen, Donna, James, and all of my fans.

I do not want to thank Aaron Sutliff for any part of this book.

A very special thanks goes out to my friends, Mr. F.G. and Mr. S.K. If it wasn't for your collective inability to be just a little bit flexible and allow my daughters to finish up the school year prior to my relocation to Savannah, I would still be in the Army. This inflexibility and subsequent lack of integrity by both of you, put me in the position to write this brilliant piece of literature. I will always be grateful for that, and you two are the definition of what I never want to become.

Finally, I would like to thank Mike for always shooting at those who shot at me.

INTRODUCTION

Q: What do a professional athlete, a Navy SEAL, a major "player" in the music industry, an unpublished author, a surgeon, and a housewife have in common?

A: They all think this book is awesome. If you don't believe me . . . close this book, flip it over, and read the back cover.

This is my story of how to rid yourself of unwanted items, or items that maybe your wife wants to keep but really doesn't need. Craigslist is a great tool to use in order to unload the crap you don't want, but I found through trial and error that there are certain things that must be utilized in your listings in order to accomplish getting the most money for your items with the minimum amount of hassle.

I am a 13-year Army veteran. I deployed twice to Iraq and twice to Afghanistan. In September of 2011, I received orders to relocate to Savannah, Georgia. As enticing as Savannah may sound, I didn't really feel like moving to the beach just so I could go back to Afghanistan for a fifth deployment. My wife and I talked our options over and decided to get out of the Army.

Making poor decisions has never been a big issue for me. So, on a whim and with no future job in store, I submitted my paperwork to be released from Active Duty. My commitment had been fulfilled, and the Army was happy to let me go. About two months later I was offered a job with an overseas company. The job looked perfect and it would allow me to come home to my wife and kids every night while still doing the work that I enjoyed doing in the military.

One of the many issues that we faced was that it was completely impractical to move all of our belongings overseas with us. On top of that, most of the electrical items we owned would not work with the 220-volt power that was used overseas. We realized that we had to get rid of the majority of the things that we owned. Since we needed cash, and we didn't really want to just give away everything we owned, we decided to utilize craigslist.com to sell a large portion of the things we planned on leaving behind.

I posted a few things on Craigslist and was disappointed with how people would naturally haggle over the price of an item I was selling without ever actually looking at the item. This book is my story of how I learned to successfully get what I wanted for an item without ever having to negotiate the price. All items in this book sold for the asking price. So, let me tell you my secrets to selling your crap on Craigslist.

All listings in this book are the actual listings that were posted on Craigslist. They are complete with my original misspellings and grammatical errors.

This is the last item I sold. Not a Good Idea.

Whirlpool Duet Frontload Washer and Dryer Combo—$500 (Clarksville (Sango))

Date: 2012-05-28, 4:09PM EDT
Reply to: *your anonymous craigslist address will appear here*

My wife has been getting quite upset with me lately for selling all of our stuff on Craigslist. She`s even threatened to sell me on this site. But that`s not gonna stop me from posting this crazy offer! I'm selling this awesome Whirlpool Duet Frontload Washer & Dryer Combo. These are only 3 years old and they work like champs. The washer is simple to operate. First, your wife puts dirty stuff in it, adds some soap into an easy access tray, and then pushes the start button. When the washer is done washing the items inside of it, it beeps. The beep is your signal to yell for your wife to take the items out of the washer and put them in the dryer. Once she has accomplished this, with the simple push of a button, the dryer starts spinning the items inside and blows really, really hot air on them. Approximately 45 minutes later the dryer will make a beeping sound.

That sound means that you need to tell your wife or kids to take the items out of the dryer and fold them, and put them away. I love these because I do nothing but take a brief break from drinking my beer to issue verbal commands, and my clothes are clean and in my drawer . . . waiting for me to get them dirty again. So here's the deal on this: I need to keep using these until July 7 2012. So at 9:00 am on July 7, I will walk out my front door with an ice cold beer (I like to drink early on Saturday) in my hand and whoever is in my front yard can give me at least $500 and take these away. If there are multiple people in my yard, then whoever gives me the most money can have them. It will be like a really fun auction that starts at $500. My address will be posted 3 days prior to this auction. I'm about 5 minutes off of exit 11. The first 3 people to call or text me at 931-249-7016 can RSVP a parking spot in my driveway. My children will write your name with sidewalk chalk in your assigned spot. The VIP parking will open at 8:30 am. While you're waiting for this auction over the next month and a half, check out my other fine items I'm selling against my wife's wishes. Just search "931-249-7016." I'll be putting stuff up for sale every day until there is nothing left in my house.

- Location: Clarksville (Sango)
- it's NOT ok to contact this poster with services or other commercial interests

CHAPTER 1

THE FUNDAMENTALS

CHOOSE THE RIGHT VENUE

There are a few good ways to get rid of stuff and get a little bit of money. I have used several of them, and it is important to understand the pros and cons of each one. To make this simple, I'll just talk quickly about eBay and Craigslist.

Selling things on eBay is a very good way to get rid of small items that you don't want. In my opinion, it may be the best way to get the most for your money on items that you can fit into a flat rate box. What makes eBay special is that you have a world-wide sales audience. No matter what it is you have, there is somebody out there that will pay money for it. I have literally taken things out of the trash, posted them on eBay for 99 cents, and watched as people bid the price up.

One of the downsides to eBay, though, is that you have to pay 9% of the total price (sale price and shipping cost) to eBay. Additionally, there are a lot of household items that are completely impractical to ship. It's hard to mail a dining room table across the country. Another problem with eBay is that you have to pay to list your items once you go over the "monthly limit." For the most part though, eBay can get you more money than you would expect for those things you no longer need because people get into mindless bidding wars. In some cases, though, you may list an item on eBay in a bidding format, and you have a chance of getting nowhere near what it is worth. Once somebody bids on your item, unless you've put up a "reserve price", you are required to sell it for whatever price it is bid up to, even if it is only 99 cents.

Now let's talk about Craigslist since that is what this book is about. The only real downside to Craigslist when you compare it to eBay is that you are targeting a local audience of potential buyers. Because of this, you will rarely be able to get people to pay more than your item is worth. On the plus side, it is 100% free to list an item on Craigslist. Also, since everything is done locally, you can easily get rid of your refrigerator because the buyer will come get it. Since Craigslist is not set up for an auction type of sale, you can set your price and are not obligated to sell it for any less than you want.

The point here is that it is important to choose the right venue for the item which you are selling. If you are trying to sell some rare baseball card, eBay may be the better place to list it. On the flip side, if you are trying to sell a recliner, you probably won't have much luck with that on eBay, but on Craigslist you will definitely have people knocking on your door.

UNDERSTAND THE 3 DIFFERENT KINDS OF PEOPLE WHO BROWSE CRAIGSLIST

Once you have determined that Craigslist is the right place to sell your item, it is important to understand the kinds of people you may encounter by listing the item on Craigslist. I like to break down the people who shop on Craigslist into three categories. The categories are: (1) Thieves from foreign countries who have a terrible grasp of English, and who like to send emails to you hoping they can get some personal information that they can use to steal your identity and money. (2) People who have a single goal: to try to talk you down on your asking price. (3) People who know a good deal when they see one.

Category 1: The thief. This person likes to send emails in response to your ads. Usually this person's name will be very American sounding, but just by reading the email you can tell he is from somewhere far away. For instance, you may receive an email from a Michael Smith that says: "I like buy your item. Please let know if still have." If you respond to this, you will receive another email where this clown says that he will pay your asking price and the shipping costs for you to mail him the refrigerator that you listed. If you're dumb enough to respond to that email, he will then start asking for your bank account number and other information so he can supposedly wire the money directly into your account. In order to avoid wasting your time, it is easiest to just never respond to most emails. The majority of them seem to be phishing schemes, and they ultimately just waste your time.

For some reason, there are a few legitimate buyers who choose to respond to listings via email even though a phone number is included in the listing. I have found that if the email includes information that goes beyond a simple sentence asking if you still have the item or if the item is in good condition, then there is a decent chance that you are reading something from a prospective buyer and not a thief. I just use caution when responding to emails and try not to waste too much time on them.

Category 2: The haggler. In my experience with Craigslist, about half of the people who contact you will respond to your ad by asking if you'll take a lesser amount of money than you're asking. No matter what price you list your item at, these people feel the need to negotiate. It's as if they have an uncontrollable urge to try getting a better deal than they're already being offered. I've had people call me and claim that they could buy the same item brand new at Walmart for half the price for which I was selling mine. Obviously, if that was truly the case, then they wouldn't be wasting their time calling me to tell me about this bargain deal. They would be at Walmart buying the item because it is most likely mismarked. In Medical School, these people are diagnosed with cranial rectumitis which, from what I remember from Pre-Med, can only be treated with a lobotomy or euthanization (Disclaimer: I never actually became a doctor).

I have also had people try talking me down $5 on a $100 item. I sometimes have a difficult time not feeling sorry for this kind of person because it is plainly obvious that his life is a complete soup sandwich. Ultimately though, the very principle of what these people are attempting to do is reason enough to not even allow them the opportunity to buy your item.

I like to handle these people by sending patronizing and snide text messages back to them, or if they contact me with a phone call, I like to patronize them verbally. Doing that is probably not the right way to deal with them (unless you just like entertaining yourself and getting cussed at over the phone). The best way to handle these people is to ignore them or to simply tell them you're not interested. Based on my experience, a person who tries lowering the price of an item without ever seeing the item has no intention of ever paying full price. To even respond to one of these people is a complete waste of your time. The bottom line is that the "hagglers" are not your target group. Unless you are willing to lower the price of your item, just ignore them. If you have done your research on the item you are selling, then there is somebody out there that will be more than willing to pay your asking price.

Category 3: The smart person. This is the person who knows what a good deal is when he/she sees it. These are the only people with whom you should be concerned. No matter what it is that you're selling, as long as you've done your research on it and know what it is worth, there will be someone who wants it. Patience is often the key. You may have to wait a few weeks, but eventually you will get a call or text message from someone who wants to pay your asking price. You will usually be able to identify these people instantly because they actually sound excited about buying your item once they find out that it is still available. These people will never mention the price of the item unless it is just to confirm that your price isn't a misprint.

REASON FOR SELLING AND TIME CONSTRAINTS

Whatever item it is that you're selling, there is a reason you're selling it. My reason for selling things was that I needed to get rid of everything I did not want to move with me, and I needed to accomplish this within 2 months. The reason that you're selling an item and how much time you have to get it sold will play a factor in how you price it and how firm you can be in your pricing. If you are in no hurry at all to sell an item, then you may have the luxury of setting your price a little higher than somebody who needs to get rid of the item right away.

If you are reading this book with the sole purpose of getting few laughs, then I hope you're not disappointed. If you're reading this to get some pointers on selling things on Craigslist, then keep in mind that I priced my items based on my goal of getting rid of everything in a very short period of time. With that being said, don't think that you need to slash

the price of your blender by 75% of what you paid for it a year ago in order for it to sell. However, if you've had something listed on Craigslist for more than a couple of months and nobody has bought it, you may have it priced incorrectly.

CHAPTER 2

STUFF THAT PLUGS IN

This sale was the result of posting my listing on facebook. Some idiot UH-60 Instructor Pilot who I've known for years bought this. And he got a free chicken out of the deal.

Deep Freezer—$75 (Clarksville (Sango))

Date: 2012-05-14, 12:36PM EDT

Reply to: *your anonymous craigslist address will appear here*

I'm at it again!! My wife just left the house and after the backlash of listing a bunch of our furniture on Craigslist last night and pretty much selling it all this morning, I decided it would be a good idea to empty out the deep freezer and sell it. We're moving out of the country in July and I'm trying to get rid of stuff early. The price is non-negotiable and I will not hold the item. The first person who shows up to my house and gives me $75 gets to take it home. My phone has been beeping at me all morning thanks to all the awesome stuff I've been getting rid of. This deep freezer is amazing. It keeps anything you put in it frozen until you take an item out and let it thaw. It is 32 inches tall, 38 inches wide and 21 inches deep. Due to the fact that it was almost completely full and I didn't have enough freezer space between the two fridges I have . . . . this freezer comes with 1 frozen chicken. The chicken was raised by a local farmer and is pretty much organic from what I can tell. There is also a flank steak included along with some vegetarian beef patties (I'm not even sure why we have those). Additionally there are 2 jars of frozen chicken broth. The broth is fantastic . . . . it was made with smoked "organic" chicken. Call or text 931-249-7016

- Location: Clarksville (Sango)
- it's NOT ok to contact this poster with services or other commercial interests

PostingID: 3014733592

Euro Cuisine Yogurt Maker YM80—$10 (Clarksville (Sango))

Date: 2012-05-15, 9:59AM EDT
Reply to: *your anonymous craigslist address will appear here*

I'm selling my wife's Yogurt Maker!! If you love yogurt like I do, then you don't want to miss out on this great deal. I would eat yogurt all day long if I could . . . . and I have been doing that . . . which is why this item must be sold. You can buy this item online for the high price of $25. Or you can buy this one for $10. It's like new and still in the box. It's probably only been used about a dozen times. But each of those 12 times has been a moment that my family has completely cherished. We find ourselves talking about the delicious yogurt that this thing has made for us on a regular basis. $10 is my firm price. I'm selling most of the things I own, so the first person who gives me $10 gets to take this treasure home. Call or text 931-249-7016. And if you're in the market for some other fabulous kitchen appliances . . . stay tuned for more to come.

- Location: Clarksville (Sango)
- it's NOT ok to contact this poster with services or other commercial interests

PostingID: 3016544502

Hacking into my wife's Facebook account and posting this paid off almost instantly.

Food Dehydrator—Nesco Model FD-27—$10 (Clarksville (Sango))

Date: 2012-05-15, 10:36AM EDT
Reply to: *your anonymous craigslist address will appear here*

Selling off my wife's food dehydrator for her without her knowledge . . . . so we need to keep this on the down-low. It is the Nesco Model FD-27, but in my opinion should just be called "The Greatest Food Dryer In The World". This thing will dehydrate anything for you . . . . and I'm quite certain you're not just limited to food. So whatever your dehydrating needs are . . . . this is the beast that you've been searching for. It is in excellent condition and I can let you sample some dried pears to prove it's worth. $10 is a firm price and I'm selling this to the first person who gives me the $10. Call or text me at 931-249-7016. If you call within 5 minutes of reading this posting, I'll throw in a free "dum dum lollipop."

- Location: Clarksville (Sango)
- it's NOT ok to contact this poster with services or other commercial interests

PostingID: 3016617713

Sold to a friend of a person who saw this listing on my facebook page.

Automatic Bread Maker—$50 (Clarksville (Sango))

Date: 2012-05-15, 11:08AM EDT
Reply to: *your anonymous craigslist address will appear here*

I'm selling yet another one of my wife's items while she is off galavanting. I feel that if I sell things that she has, it will help pay for the things that she is probably currently buying. With that being said here is a beautiful Cuisinart CBK-200 2-Pound Convection Automatic Bread Maker. If

you're into eating bread and magic tricks then you want this item! All you do is mix together a bunch of ingredients and then stick them in this bread maker and shortly thereafter the bread maker will make a beeping noise. When you here this noise, you open the lid and then there is a loaf of delicious bread waiting to be eaten. Amazon sells this thing for $122.26. I'm only asking for $50 because that will cover perhaps half of the price of the shoes that my wife is currently buying. This is a firm price and I'm confident this item will be sold by the end of the day. I won't hold it for you so quickly text or call me at 931-249-7016.

- Location: Clarksville (Sango)
- it's NOT ok to contact this poster with services or other commercial interests

PostingID: 3016686531

Yet another reason to have the password to your wife's facebook account. She has so many friends who like to buy stupid chick stuff.

Seal-A-Meal VS106 Vacuum Food Sealer—$50 (Clarksville (Sango))

Date: 2012-05-16, 8:37PM EDT
Reply to: *your anonymous craigslist address will appear here*

So my wife was yelling at me again today for selling off our deep freezer earlier this week. She can't seem to grasp the fact that I'm addicted to selling stuff . . . even if it means we have nothing and make just a fraction of what it's worth. So since I sold the deep freezer, she told me that she was about to vacuum seal some produce and then try to find a place to cram it into the now packed freezer in our kitchen. I'm having none of that!!!! I'm now listing her Seal-A-Meal VS106 Vacuum Food Sealer. You can buy this thing new on amazon.com for $111.00 or you can pick it up used on Amazon for $66. I'm undercutting Amazon at $50 and then destroying my wife's will to fight my selling spree with this unbeatable offer. And let me just tell you a thing or two about this vacuum sealer. It's top-of-the-line!!!

All of the frozen goodies that she's been hoarding away in the deep freezer are now rotting in our backyard and I can't smell a thing! This is one amazing product! Call fast because this won't be around for long. You can text or call me at 931-249-7016. I'm practically giving this baby away, but to sweeten the deal even more, I'm including two boxes of already-opened-but-mostly-full vacuum sealer bags. I have no idea what these bags would cost you at the store, but I'm almost positive they cost more than "free". So come buy a vacuum sealer and drive your husband crazy by buying more produce and meats than you need and then filling a deep freezer up just in case a nuclear holocaust is in the future. As with everything I'm selling, this price is non-negotiable and the first person to give me the money gets the sealer. And if you're looking to buy more of my wife's crap, search my phone number in Craigslist.

- Location: Clarksville (Sango)
- it's NOT ok to contact this poster with services or other commercial interests

PostingID: 3020071043

4 hours after listing this, somebody came and picked it up. And I was wondering how I was going to get this to the dump.

55" Television—Mitsubishi WS-55413—$50 (Clarksville (Sango))

Date: 2012-05-26, 10:03AM EDT
Reply to: *your anonymous craigslist address will appear here*

My wife told me last night that we no longer have beer left in our budget, so if I want to continue drinking 12 beers a day, I need to find a new source of income. Because of her inability to compromise in a mature manner, I'm taking the "high road" and selling this fully functioning 55" television for the incredibly low price of $50. This thing works great. It's only 8 years old and if you have an operational time machine, you could go back to the year 2004 and buy this for $1500. Or, you could save your plutonium stock and $1450 and buy it from me for $50. I don't envy you on the decision you have to make on that one. This is an HD 1080i projection television with a ton of inputs. It works great for a gaming TV, which is what my kids use it for (they're gonna be a little upset with me on this). This is not one of those new-style-feminine-slim televisions. This is a manly television that takes up a ton of space and weighs about as much as a refrigerator. Plus it has wheels with an almost zero-turn radius. I can't say enough about how great this thing is. Just like everything else I'm selling, my price is fixed and the first person to give me $50 can take this home. Call or text 931-249-7016, and while you're at it, check out the other awesome stuff I'm getting rid of by searching "7016".

- Location: Clarksville (Sango)
- it's NOT ok to contact this poster with services or other commercial interests

PostingID: 3039088446

My wife's Facebook page helped sell this one almost instantly.

Food Processor—Hamilton Beach—70450—$15 (Clarksville (Sango)

Date: 2012-05-26, 10:33AM EDT
Reply to: *your anonymous craigslist address will appear here*

Unbeknownst to my wife, I'm selling off another one of her prized possessions. I've been trying to get my family on a strictly fast-food diet and this thing is getting in the way of my goal. Because of this fine item, and the food it processes so well, my kids have far too much energy and are driving me crazy. I'm hoping that by forcing the family to eat at McDonalds everyday and consume a diet loaded up with MSG, they will become more lethargic and leave me alone. This food processor will process any item you put into it in a matter of seconds. It has a whole bunch of really sharp blades that cut up and shred whatever kind of food you cram into it. It also comes with the highly coveted "pulse" mode. The pulse mode not only sounds cool, but it helps when processing things that should never be put into the food processor to begin with. As far as I can tell, this thing is in pretty much perfect shape. I believe my wife paid around $50 for this so in order to come up with a "can't say no" price, I got rid of the zero after the five and then placed a one before the five and came up with the $15 price (that's how this beautiful mind works). That's a pretty much unbeatable price and if you call or text me at 931-249-7016, this can be yours. The price is firm and if you're looking for some more great kitchen appliances, search "7016" to see what else I'm getting rid of.

- • Location: Clarksville (Sango)
- • it's NOT ok to contact this poster with services or other commercial interests

PostingID: 3039138321

I was really surprised that I was able to sell these in the middle of the summer. Two people called me about a week after I listed it but they never showed up like they said they would. Then about a week later I got a text message from someone who said he wanted them and sure enough . . . he showed up and gave me my 40 dollars.

Portable Heater / Fan—Lasko—Model 755320—$40 (Clarksville (Sango))

Date: 2012-05-28, 4:09PM EDT
Reply to: *your anonymous craigslist address will appear here*

I'm selling a bundle of two (2) (dos) Lasko 755320 Ceramic Tower Heaters with Digital Display and one (1) (uno) Remote Control. "Remote Control" is singular because I lost one of them . . . but don't worry . . . . the one I have will control both. These heater/fans are amazing. Now that the temperature has dropped well below 80 degrees at night, you can snuggle up to this thing and stay warm and cozy all night long . . . . or with the use of the remote control you can instantly switch this to "fan" mode and have unheated air blown directly on your face. I can't say enough about this item. It actually tears me up to sell these. You can buy one of these brand new with one remote on Amazon right now for $56. That's outrageous compared to paying me only $40 for 2 (two) (dos) of these and one (1) (uno) remote. So you get the same amount of remotes but double the heater/fans!!! Unbelievable. Call or text me at 931-249-7016 if you're interested . . . and since you've read this far, I can only assume you're interested or you're just waiting for me to type something stupid (which isn't gonna happen). This price is firm and as always, the first person who gives me the money gets the merchandise . . . so don't ask me to hold anything for you . . . . I'm selling everything in my house in less than a month utilizing Craigslist only!!! So stay tuned for more awesome stuff!!!

- Location: Clarksville (Sango)
- it's NOT ok to contact this poster with services or other commercial interests

PostingID: 3018275038

This one took a little over a week before I was able to offload it.

Presto 08800 EverSharp Electric Knife Sharpener—$10 (Clarksville (Sango))

Date: 2012-05-28, 4:24PM EDT
Reply to: *your anonymous craigslist address will appear here*

My wife has been getting a tad upset over the past couple of weeks because I've been selling her kitchen appliances without letting her know. In order to remedy this misunderstanding, last night we had a conversation that went like this (this is my version of the conversation only): "Woman! Go sharpen the knives right now!" "Why should I do that, my awesome husband?" "Because I'm gonna sell the stupid thing on Craigslist!"

So she instantly sharpened the knives and then like an obedient wife she started preparing dinner. While cutting the green stuff off of the top of some strawberries (cuz that's the way I like them prepared), she sliced her finger almost to the bone! I'm telling this story as a testament to how awesome this knife sharpener is. We have some crappy knives, yet this Presto knife sharpener will work it's magic and sharpen pretty much anything that is made of metal.

I don't want to get all scientific on you, but this thing has sapphirite sharpening wheels which create a perfect, razor sharp edge in just seconds. If you don't believe me, stop by my house and look at the wound under my wife's Dora the Explorer Band-Aid. This is the real deal. Plus, this sharpener has precision blade guides that automatically hold the knife at the perfect sharpening angle. Additionally, it has a 2-stage sharpening system. The first stage "grinds" and the second stage "hones." As far as I know, you can't get a perfectly sharpened knife without grinding and honing.

So, I'm selling this beast for the low price of $10. If that doesn't sound like a fair price, then you should go online and buy it for $40 (and then punch yourself in the face for being an idiot and wasting money). I'm selling everything in my house and these items are going fast. Text or call me at 931-249-7016. The price is firm and the first person to give me $10 gets this precious little tool. Search "7016" if you'd like to see the other awesome stuff I'm selling.

- Location: Clarksville (Sango)
- it's NOT ok to contact this poster with services or other commercial interests

PostingID: 3043104783

Nobody contacted me about this for 10 days, and then all of a sudden, two people called me about it within a 10 minute period. The first guy who showed up to my house got it and I got 40 bucks.

DVD Surround System—JVC—TH-M45—$40 (Clarksville (Sango))

Date: 2012-05-28, 10:04PM EDT
Reply to: *your anonymous craigslist address will appear here*

Due to the fact that I had a temporary case of tunnel vision and sold my 55" television for $50 so I could buy some beer, I now have no reason to keep this DVD Surround System. Thankfully, I just recently converted all of my dvd's to VHS format in order to save space, so the DVD player would have been no use to me anyway. These are the reasons that I'm selling this killer Surround Sound System for $40. Let me just tell you a thing or two about this system. First, they don't make them like this anymore (at least not in the last 7 years). Second, this classy system has a 5-disc dvd changer with direct digital progressive scan. It has a subwoofer and 5 surround sound speakers. It also comes with both AM and FM antennas (pretty sweet) and a remote control (that works). And if you're into burning mp3's on to CD-R's (because listening to them on your iphone is for poor people), this system allows you to play mp3 CD's as well. It's quite amazing. What's even more amazing than the $40 price for this impressive system, is the fact that I'm throwing in an 8-pack of 6X 1 3/4" Flat Phillips Wood Screws free of charge. These screws are great for screwing things together and I no longer need them because I accidentally sold my cordless screw driver last week for $30 because I ran out of beer again. My price is non-negotiable as always and if you're interested in more awesome stuff so I can continue drinking around the clock, then search "7016" and check out my other listings. Text or Call 931-249-7016.

- Location: Clarksville (Sango)
- it's NOT ok to contact this poster with services or other commercial interests

PostingID: 3039970443

A few days after listing this, a woman called me and asked me if I would take $40 since "she had to drive all the way to my house." I'm guessing that kind of logic doesn't work for her when she shops at the mall. I kindly told her that I wasn't interested. Nobody called about this again until I got an email about 2 weeks later from a woman in the hospital who wanted it but had no way of getting it until she was released from the hospital. So my daughters and I took a "field trip" to the hospital to visit her and bring her the sewing machine. She had just had a heart attack, but she snuck down to the lobby of the hospital to get $50 out of the ATM. I had the money in my hands, but I couldn't take it. I gave it back to her and told her that she could pay me once she got out of the hospital.

Sewing Machine—Brother LS-590—$50 (Clarksville (Sango))

Date: 2012-05-30, 12:28AM EDT
Reply to: *your anonymous craigslist address will appear here*

I'm selling my wife's sewing machine. She bought this less than a year ago when I was out of town and I don't think she even knows how to sew. I just found it today when I was rooting through her stuff, looking for beer money. I didn't find any money, so I will turn this into money. This sewing machine is perhaps the best sewing machine on the market for $100. It is compatible with every color of thread and it has a lot of different knobs and buttons on it. These knobs and buttons each have their own special function which you can read about in the manual that you will get when you buy this. According to the writing on the side of this thing, it is jam resistant due to the drop-in top bobbin. I don't know a single thing about sewing machines, but I don't think I would ever buy one without a drop-in top bobbin . . . not in this day-and-age at least. This baby also has a "brightly lit work area", just in case you want to sew in the dark. A few of the other features worth mentioning are the built-in free arm and the built-in threading system along with the quick-change presser feet. You can read all about this on the side of the sewing machine (just like I'm doing right now) when you come to my house to buy it.

I will not take less than $50 so don't even ask and the first person to get here and give me the money gets the machine. Call or text 931-249-7016. I'm selling everything I own on Craigslist in less than 2 months, so search "7016" to see what else I'm selling.

- Location: Clarksville (Sango)
- it's NOT ok to contact this poster with services or other commercial interests

PostingID: 3036530101

This was sold because a nice older lady was getting enjoyment out of reading my other listings. She found this and figured her son would want it.

Blender—Hamilton Beach—54200R—$5 (Clarksville (Sango))

Date: 2012-05-31, 3:56PM EDT
Reply to: *your anonymous craigslist address will appear here*

This is the Hamilton Beach 54200R Blender. You can no longer buy this blender in stores because it was discontinued a few years ago. I have no way of backing this claim up, but I have heard that they discontinued this model because they were selling too many of them and the production line could not keep up with the demand. Because of this, they were forced to start manufacturing blenders that were less reliable than the 54200R. Basically, this thing is a treasure and the $5 price is incredible, especially since it is on the verge of attaining "antique" status. Due to the fact that this is, in my opinion, the best blender in the world, it obviously still works like new. It has an almost unlimited amount of blending modes. It will "Grate", "Grind", "Beat", "Shred", "Blend", "Liquefy", "Frappe", "Stir", "Aerate", "Puree", "Crumb", "Chop", and "Mix". In addition to all of these complex modes, it also has the "ice breaker" mode. Hurry and text or call me at 931-249-7016 so you can get here before anyone else buys it first. If you want to see the other kitchen appliances I'm selling, search 7016.

- Location: Clarksville (Sango)
- it's NOT ok to contact this poster with services or other commercial interests

PostingID: 3049364492

I was surprised that it took 2 weeks before anyone called me about this. Finally a really cool couple with their young daughter came over to pick it up and we actually hung out for a bit while our kids played together.

KitchenAid KSM150PSMC Artisan Series 5-Quart Mixer, Metallic Chrome—$200 (Clarksville (Sango))

Date: 2012-05-31, 4:55PM EDT

Reply to: *your anonymous craigslist address will appear here*

This here is the "grand daddy" of my wife's beloved kitchen appliances that I'm selling for her while she cries in our room. This mixer is the bomb!! It is the KitchenAid KSM150PSMC Artisan Series 5-Quart Mixer. It comes in a beautiful Metallic Chrome color (if you're not happy with that color, I'll throw in a free can of spray paint so you can give it the Krylon touch when you get it back to your house. Let me just tell you a little about how this thing works and what it can do for you: it is a 325-watt mixer with 10 speeds (super slow to super fast). It comes with a 5-quart stainless steel bowl and a tilt-back head for easy access to the stuff you're mixing. It has a 2-piece pouring shield with a large chute for adding ingredients and it includes a flat beater, dough hook, and wire whip. This thing is great for people who want to feel like a real baker while mixing together a box of Betty Crocker cake mix. I'm sure it can be used by a real baker, but I have yet to see that. Amazon is having a sale on this so if you go right now to amazon.com you can buy this brand new $329.99. If that's a little too rich for your blood, then you can buy it used at Amazon for $261.99. Or just come to my house and give me $200 and you can use it tonight instead of waiting for it to get shipped to you. This thing is in almost perfect condition and my price is firm. Text or call me at 931-249-7016. Check out my other fine kitchen appliances that I'm selling by searching "7016".

- Location: Clarksville (Sango)
- it's NOT ok to contact this poster with services or other commercial interests

PostingID: 3049497122

Hamilton Beach 45234 Stay or Go Thermal Coffee Maker—$15 (Clarksville (Sango))

Date: 2012-06-10, 9:42AM EDT
Reply to: *your anonymous craigslist address will appear here*

I don't drink coffee and my wife just left town for a few days. What this means is that she won't be needing this until Thursday morning at the earliest. This may be the best coffee maker on the market for $60 . . . . and it can be yours for only $15 if you get here before Thursday. Besides making coffee, this thing has a digital clock on the front. The clock is the only feature on this coffee maker that I have ever used and it works great. I absolutely love waking up in the morning and looking at this fine coffee maker and instantly knowing what time it is. The clock feature on this thing is worth the $15 by itself. So if you like coffee, and knowing what time it is, then this is the item you've been searching for. Text or call me at 931-249-7016. My price is firm and if you want to see what else I'm selling, search "7016"

- Location: Clarksville (Sango)
- it's NOT ok to contact this poster with services or other commercial interests

PostingID: 3068747730

My friend Larissa bought this one afternoon when she stopped by my house to give me a half-rack of beer and pick up some clothes I was giving away. She saw this beauty sitting on the floor and couldn't pass up the $5 bargain.

Presto PopLite Hot Air Popcorn Popper, 04820—$5 (Clarksville (Sango))

Date: 2012-06-10, 10:29AM EDT

Reply to: *your anonymous craigslist address will appear here*

If you're into popcorn like I am . . . . this is the popper you want. This bad boy can pop some corn and melt some butter all at once. It is in great shape and less than 3 months old. My wife had to purchase this one because our old one actually blew up because I over filled it when I was on one of my popcorn binges. We upgraded to this heavy duty beast because electrical fires aren't fun. $20 is what Walmart is selling this for. My firm price is $5 but to sweeten the deal even more, I'm including a bag of popcorn that is mostly full. I know that Craigslist people have been known to kill people in the past, so if you're worried about the possibility of me poisoning this bag of popcorn, I will pop up a batch of popcorn in front of you and you can pick one of my daughters to eat the popcorn. We can sit and observe her for up to an hour to make sure she doesn't start vomiting or bleeding from the nose. Once you are satisfied, you can hand me my $5 and take the popcorn and the popper home. Call or text me at 931-249-7016. If you'd like to see what else I'm selling, search "7016."

- Location: Clarksville (Sango)
- it's NOT ok to contact this poster with services or other commercial interests

PostingID: 3068808813

I had two people racing to my house to get this the day after I listed it. One was disappointed.

Magnavox DVD Player—Model DP170MW8B—$5 (Clarksville (Sango))

Date: 2012-06-10, 2:51PM EDT

Reply to: *your anonymous craigslist address will appear here*

This is a used Magnavox DVD Player. It has both RCA and HDMI Inputs and it has been used about 10 times. It works great and has a working remote. I love this thing but I just recently converted all of my DVD's to VHS in order to save space so I no longer have a need for it. Text or Call 931-249-7016 and check out my other listings by searching "7016".

- Location: Clarksville (Sango)
- it's NOT ok to contact this poster with services or other commercial interests

PostingID: 3069279716

CHAPTER 3

MONEY STUFF

BE REALISTIC ON YOUR PRICING
AND DO SOME RESEARCH

By the very nature of the website, people shop on Craigslist because they want to find the lowest price on whatever it is they are looking to buy. This is something that you can use to your advantage by making your price just a little bit lower than anybody else's. Most likely you're selling a used item. It is important to be realistic and to do a little bit of research. Amazon.com is a great place to find prices for both new and used items. If the item you're selling isn't on Amazon then just do a Google search and you will most likely find it. It takes less than a minute and you can figure out exactly how much a person can expect to pay for the same item you're selling. If you make your price a little lower than the competition's price, you will almost be guaranteed to sell it. Also, search Craigslist to see for what other people in the area are selling similar items. Undercut them by about 10%, and your item will be the one that people choose to buy.

If you are selling something that is "out of season", you may be better off waiting until it is "in season". If you don't have that luxury, then be prepared to list it for a lower price than you would actually like to get. For instance, if you choose to sell an electric blanket in July, you are going to have a very hard time finding a person who is shopping for a warm blanket in the summer. You just have to be realistic about what it is you're selling and what somebody will actually pay for it.

If you're selling an expensive item, you may have to cut the price quite a bit in order to sell it. For instance, if you're selling a $2000 sofa that you bought five years ago, you probably won't be able to get $1500 for it. It is possible, but you have to find the person who is looking for that exact sofa. When you think about it, you bought your bedroom set because you shopped around and found the bedroom set that fit your house and fit your style. People on Craigslist who are in the market for a bedroom set will most likely neither have the means nor the willingness to pay several thousand dollars for this. If they did, they would be at a furniture shop instead of shopping on Craigslist.

The gist of it all is that you have to be realistic when it comes to your item's selling price. People take a risk buying things on Craigslist because they can't take the item back and there is no warranty. If you're selling something on Craigslist with the intention of finding a "sucker" who will pay you more than it's worth, then good luck. My goal for everything I sold was always to get my targeted amount of money which would result in me getting rid of an item that I no longer wanted. If I was happy and the buyer was happy, then I felt that it was a great transaction.

NO OBO

I have seen a lot of listings on Craigslist where the seller lists the price and then follows it with OBO (Or Best Offer). I can only think of three reasons why somebody would list an item this way. (1) They have no idea what it is worth, and they have just randomly attached a price to their listing. (2) They actually want people to haggle with them because idiots like talking to other idiots. (3) They expect people to negotiate the price, so they set the price at a higher value than they really expect, knowing that the price will get talked down.

To me, it really makes no sense to not say exactly what you want for the item you're selling. If you list something with OBO attached to a price, you are guaranteed to not get your asking price. All you have done is given a buyer a number from which to negotiate. That is the same as saying "I will take no more than $500 for this table." You're pretty much asking somebody to give you less money than you want. I understand that some people like to set a price higher than they actually want because they expect to do a negotiating dance. I feel, however, that it is in everybody's best interest to just be a "man" about it and say exactly how much you want for the item you're selling.

FIRM PRICE

With that being said, make your price "firm." You know how much the item that you are selling is worth because you did your research, and you know exactly what somebody will have to pay for the same item somewhere else. Craigslist buyers love to call you up and start negotiating. They will gladly talk down your asking price by over 50% without ever seeing the item. In order to dismiss these idiots, it is vital to list your item's price as "non-negotiable" or "firm". You will still get phone calls from a few morons who either did not read the full ad or are just too dense to understand what "firm" means. Ultimately, by saying in your ad that your price is "firm" you will weed out the majority of the people who are just looking to negotiate the price and waste your time.

CASH ONLY

Cash should be the only form of payment you accept in your transactions. I personally won't accept cashier's checks or money orders because there are people out there who have been known to hand out fake ones. I have accepted personal checks on two occasions, but I knew both people personally. With the easy accessibility to ATM's and banks, I can't think of a good reason why a person would not have the ability to bring you cash. If you're selling something very expensive like a car, you probably won't have much choice but to accept a cashier's check. Just be smart about it and have the buyer meet you at your bank and have the check or money order deposited into your account before you hand over the keys.

CHAPTER 4

FURNITURE

This is the first item I sold. It was gone within a week. A school teacher bought it and she was happier than a pig in poo.

Hamilton Piano—$250 (Clarksville (Sango))

Date: 2012-05-08, 3:40PM EDT

Reply to: *your anonymous craigslist address will appear here*

This is a Hamilton Piano with a bench. The bench is full of piano music. I don't know much about pianos at all, but this one seems to work and is in decent condition. There are a couple of cosmetic issues, but for the most part, it looks good. I'm selling this because my kids do not know how to play a piano; however, their lack of knowledge does not prevent them from constantly playing it. I hate this piano. The noise it makes can be very painful. So you can have it for the low price of $250 bucks . . . . that almost covers the cost I paid for it 2 years ago, but it will never cover the emotional damage I have incurred because of children who have no idea how to play it. The thing is heavy . . . so you're gonna have to come up with a plan to move it. Call or text me at 9312497016.

- Location: Clarksville (Sango)
- it's NOT ok to contact this poster with services or other commercial interests

PostingID: 2999685171

I listed this at 10pm while drinking beer and almost instantly I got a text from a woman who wanted to pick them up at 7am the next morning. At 6am the next morning, I got a text from someone who wanted to pick them up at 8am. At 7am, the bar stools were gone and I had $50.

Bar Stools—Set of 3—They Swivel—$50 (Clarksville (Sango))

Date: 2012-05-13, 8:55PM EDT
Reply to: *your anonymous craigslist address will appear here*

My family and I are getting ready to move to a far away land and because of this, we're selling almost everything for incredibly low (non-negotiable) prices. For the low, low price of $50 you can get these 3 swiveling bar stools. They're made of metal and some sort of fabric. They're actually really nice (almost new) bar stools that we purchased from Target about 2 years ago for $70 a piece. They haven't had much use (they just sit at the bar and look cool for the most part). These stools come from a smoke free and flatulence free home . . . . so you can be assured that there will be no unwanted odors on your stools (No pun intended). $50 is my firm price and I'm selling them to the first person who gives me $50. Call or text 931-249-7016. Additionally, the dog on the floor of the second picture is not dead . . . he's just sleeping . . . and he's free to a good home. So come get some bar stools and a dog who sleeps 23 hours a day.

- Location: Clarksville (Sango)
- it's NOT ok to contact this poster with services or other commercial interests

PostingID: 3013760347

This was gone within a couple of hours of listing it. Craigslist peeps are animals!

Table w/ 4 Chairs—$50 (Clarksville (Sango))

Date: 2012-05-13, 9:09PM EDT
Reply to: *your anonymous craigslist address will appear here*

My family and I are moving in the very near future to a place where tables aren't allowed. Because of this I'm being forced to sell my most prized possession for the incredibly low price of $50. This is a "firm" price as I hate haggling. The table is in decent condition and the chairs have a few stains but no real damage. One chair is red, one is green, one is yellow and one is blue. They look awesome and I've had so many compliments on this table and the chairs. The chairs are probably the main reason my wife and daughters love me. I absolutely hate getting rid of this for only $50, but it has to be done. The table and chairs come from a smoke free home and if you call me within 15 minutes of reading this posting, I'll throw in a free deck of "bee" casino playing cards. That's how serious I am. Call or text 931-249-7016.

- Location: Clarksville (Sango)
- it's NOT ok to contact this poster with services or other commercial interests

PostingID: 3013779133

Another item that was listed late at night. Prior to 7am the next day I received a phone call from someone who wanted to buy the sofa and a few other items I had listed.

Black Leather Couch/Sofa—$200 (Clarksville/Sango)

Date: 2012-05-13, 9:10PM EDT
Reply to: *your anonymous craigslist address will appear here*

Ok . . . here we go again . . . . I'm selling everything I own because I'm moving to a foreign land with my wife and kids. All prices are non-negotiable (unless you wanna pay me more than I'm asking).

Basically . . . I'm dumping my belongings off for dirt cheap prices and I don't feel like wasting time haggling. Usually when I list an item I get at least 5 text messages within the first hour . . . . I will not promise an item to anyone. If you're the first person to show up to my house . . . and if you pay me the money I'm asking . . . . then you get the item. This is an awesome black leather couch. I paid $3000 for this couch 7 years ago. It's in excellent condition and I break down in a hysterical tantrum every time I think of selling it. This couch is so incredibly comfortable . . . . it's an insult to this couch that I'm selling it for $200. If you're interested . . . then quickly text or call me at 931-249-7016. If you act now, I'll throw in a free deck of "bee" casino playing cards. That should show how serious I am.

- Location: Clarksville (Sango)
- it's NOT ok to contact this poster with services or other commercial interests

PostingID: 2998806206

I listed these late at night and they were sold first thing in the morning.

Book Shelf—2 for 1 Sale—$30 (Clarksville (Sango))

Date: 2012-05-14, 12:02AM EDT
Reply to: *your anonymous craigslist address will appear here*

Ok . . . here we go again . . . . I'm selling everything I own because I'm moving to a foreign land with my wife and kids. All prices are non-negotiable (unless you wanna pay me more than I'm asking). Basically . . . I'm dumping my belongings off for dirt cheap prices and I don't feel like wasting time haggling. Usually when I list an item I get at least 5 text messages within the first hour . . . . I will not promise an item to anyone. If you're the first person to show up to my house . . . and if you pay me the money I'm asking . . . . then you get the item. With that being said . . . I'm selling 2 (two) 6 ft tall book shelves. I was going to ask for $30 per book shelf . . . but then I decided to be nice and give both away for $30. They are in excellent condition and my wife has no idea I'm doing this. In the pictures, there are items on the shelves . . . . those items are not included in this purchase. If you are interested in these, then I will need you to come by between the hours of 9 am and 4 pm in order to keep my wife in the dark. If you want these awesome bookshelves, then text or call me at 931-249-7016.

- Location: Clarksville (Sango)
- it's NOT ok to contact this poster with services or other commercial interests

PostingID: 3013973673

This sold within 2 hours of listing it.

Bookshelf—$10 (Clarksville (Sango))

Date: 2012-05-17, 7:33AM EDT
Reply to: *your anonymous craigslist address will appear here*

I'm starting my 2nd night of selling stuff without my wife's knowledge. It's so fun to see her reaction in the morning as strangers show up to our door and then walk out with some of our most treasured belongings. This has to been done though since we're moving to a different country in less than 2 months. So to kick things off tonight . . . I'm selling this beautiful bookshelf for the low price of just $10. As always, the price is firm and the first person who shows up at my door and gives me the money gets the bookshelf. The book shelf is just over 41 inches tall and just over 24 inches wide. It is truly a fabulous piece furniture. Next to my flat screen television, this is probably my favorite thing I own. I absolutely love it. The items on the bookshelf in the picture are not a part of this transaction . . . they're only there to demonstrate how versatile this bookshelf is. It doesn't just hold books . . . it will hold whatever you put on it. So if you're interested, text or call me at 931-249-7016. I'll respond to text messages after 6am.

- Location: Clarksville (Sango)
- it's NOT ok to contact this poster with services or other commercial interests

PostingID: 3015961546

I didn't get a single call about this for 2 weeks. Then one day somebody text messaged me and an hour later she showed up to my house with 10 bucks and took this thing home.

Desk Chair—Awesome!!!—$10 (Clarksville (Sango))

Date: 2012-05-28, 4:09PM EDT
Reply to: *your anonymous craigslist address will appear here*

I'm selling my daughter's desk chair. This needs to be done discretely however. She's at school from about 7 am until 3 pm. She loves this chair . . . but I love it more. In the morning as soon as she leaves for school, I go into her room and sit on this chair. It's so comfortable!!! I absolutely love it. Its spins around in circles and it's orange . . . which is my 3rd favorite color. This chair is in excellent condition and you could buy it new for well over $30.00 . . . and by that, I mean $31.00. I'm willing to sell her chair, that her grandmother bought her, to you for the low price of $10. Text or Call me at 931-249-7016 and we'll arrange for you to come by the house between the hours of 7 and 3 to view and test drive this modern wonder!!! Call before tomorrow and I'll throw in a free coozie (a blue one). As with all of my listings on here, the price is non-negotiable and I will not hold the item for you. This isn't because I'm a jerk . . . but rather because a large amount of Craigslist people are complete flakes. So the first person to give me ten bucks gets to take this wonderful chair home with them.

- Location: Clarksville (Sango)
- it's NOT ok to contact this poster with services or other commercial interests

PostingID: 3018232436

Dining Room Table with 8 Chairs—$250 (Clarksville (Sango))

Date: 2012-05-28, 4:09PM EDT

Reply to: *your anonymous craigslist address will appear here*

So I found out the other day that my spleen is the size of a volleyball and is pushing into my left lung and it may have to be removed. Because of that minorly inconvenient discovery, I had temporarily put the sale of all of my belongings on hold. But 5 minutes ago, I decided to just keep on selling stuff. So here's a great deal for you. This is a solid wood dining room table with 8 solid wood chairs. The table comes with two leafs and has just been refinished by me. It looks amazing. Everytime I see this table I compliment myself (out loud) about how awesome it looks. The chairs need to be refinished and I was going to do that, but then my spleen started hurting again. But back to the table: This table is great! It's a completely multi-purpose table. You can eat on it, or color on it, or do homework on it. The options are unlimited and I've never seen a table quite like it. And to top it off: it looks awesome. Because of the fact that I'm ignoring my health issues and continuing on with my plan to leave the country and sell everything for dirt cheap prices, this item can be yours for the low price of $250. If you were to buy this same table somewhere else, you would pay thousands!!! My price is "on your deathbed" low and non-negotiable. Due to the fact that a decent amount of Craigslist people tend to be flakes, I will not hold it for you . . . So the first person that comes to my house and gives me $250 can take this beauty home. Call or text me at 931-249-7016. And if you're in the market for more great deals, search "7016" and you can see what I currently have up for sale.

- Location: Clarksville (Sango)
- it's NOT ok to contact this poster with services or other commercial interests

PostingID: 3034361871

Dressers and bookshelves are the easiest things to sell. I sold one of these within an hour of listing it on the other one I made a mistake with by pulling the listing for someone I knew. To my surprise, she never returned my call when I called to ask her if she still wanted it. So I reposted the item and it sold about an hour later. Don't hold items for people!

Dresser—I have 2 of these—$20 (Clarksville (Sango))

Date: 2012-05-31, 2:06PM EDT
Reply to: *your anonymous craigslist address will appear here*

I'm selling my daughter's dressers for $20 apiece. Or if you'd like to buy both of them then I'll drop the price down to $40 total. These dressers are unique in the fact that they're both in my house and they're both full of clothes because nobody but me knows that they're for sale. Prior to your purchasing of these, the clothes will be removed and my kids will be living out of cardboard boxes for the next month or so. Should be good times. These dressers are about 4ft tall (maybe a little smaller) and they have 4 drawers. The drawers have handles to help with the opening and closing of the drawers. The dressers also have a top. The top of the dresser can be used to pile things on it instead of just putting things away I like I asked. This is obviously a "killer" deal and these won't be around for long. Quickly text or call me at 931-249-7016. You can see the other items I'm selling on here by searching "7016". The price is firm and the first person to get here and give me the money gets to take these home.

PostingID: 3049101505

It took 3 days before someone decided to buy this.

Desk—Student Desk—$15 (Clarksville (Sango))

Date: 2012-05-31, 2:17PM EDT
Reply to: *your anonymous craigslist address will appear here*

After today, the only thing my daughter will have left in her room is a bed. And she probably won't have that much longer if I keep listing her items here at the rate I have been. This desk is white and it looks incredible. It's probably one of the nicer desks I have ever seen. This is a perfect desk for your kid to sit at and do homework or to just sit at because you're busy watching TV and you don't want to deal with children at the moment. It has a drawer thing to put stuff in and it has some little shelves and a large work area to do homework or to color by number on. My wife bought this for way more than $15 . . . so my firm asking price is a stellar deal. Just text or call me at 931-249-7016. I have about 40 days left to sell everything in my house so more items will be up for sale each day.

PostingID: 3049127869

I was kind of worried about being able to sell this because not many people are in the market for a large bean bag. I had multiple people call me up and ask if I would take less than $100. I held out though and about 10 days later, a lady and her daughters showed up and were thrilled to take it off my hands for my asking price. It took about 20 minutes to stuff this in the back of her van.

6ft Comfy Sack Bean Bag—$100 (Clarksville (Sango))

Date: 2012-05-31, 2:33PM EDT
Reply to: *your anonymous craigslist address will appear here*

I'm selling one of my most prized possessions here. This is a 6 foot Bean Bag made by comfysacks.com. Anybody who knows anything about bean bags knows that comfysack is at the top of the bean bag food chain. This thing is not only comfortable to sleep on, but it has a micro-suede cover that looks super cool and feels nice. 4 kids or two adults and 4 kids can fit comfortably on this together. It also has the ability to serve many purposes (ie. couch, bed, trampoline, recliner). This item comes from a smoke free home and it has never been urinated on or farted on. It pretty much smells new and is just an amazingly comfortable piece of furniture to sit or sleep on. I bought this less than a year ago for $350 because a bean bag seemed like a smart investment . . . especially for that low price. Don't pass up on this $100 firm offer. Text or call me at 931-249-7016. Don't forget to look at the other items I'm selling by searching "7016".

- Location: Clarksville (Sango)
- it's NOT ok to contact this poster with services or other commercial interests

PostingID: 3049166538

I almost threw these in my fire pit. Within 5 minutes of posting the listing, a woman was on her way to my house to buy them.

Console Table and End Tables—$15 (Clarksville (Sango))

Date: 2012-05-31, 10:43AM EDT
Reply to: *your anonymous craigslist address will appear here*

This is Webster's definition for rustic: rus·tic (rstk) adj. a. Lacking refinement or elegance; coarse. b. Charmingly simple or unsophisticated. 3. Made of unfinished or roughly finished wood: rustic furniture. 4. Having a rough or textured appearance; rusticated. Used of masonry.

I would like to add one thing to the definition and that would be "lack of attention to detail by the builder"

I'm selling this incredibly rustic console table with matching end tables. I personally built these with saws and hammers and other manly tools about a year ago. They are made of solid wood and they look totally awesome!!! The console table can be used to put stuff on like plants and other girly stuff that your wife wants to display. The shelf on the console table can be used to hide crap that your wife leaves laying out all the time. Once you have everything on the shelves, you push your couch in front of the table and then everything is hidden except for the plants and stuff your wife wants displayed for all to see. Then about a month later your wife will ask you if you've seen some item that she can't find. Even though you know for sure that it is on the hidden shelf of the console table, you need to tell her that you don't know where it is. After she spends a couple of days, moping around the house because she can't find this item that she apparently cares so much about but didn't even know it was missing for over a month, you can safely throw it in the trash or just sell it on Craigslist. This will free up the hidden shelf for more of her crap she leaves laying around. $15 is a steal for this magical-item-eating piece of furniture. Plus it's rustic which is really cool these days. If you're interested, text or call, 931-249-7016. $15 is my firm price, which means I won't take less. If you want to buy more of my stuff I'm selling, search "7016".

- Location: Clarksville (Sango)
- it's NOT ok to contact this poster with services or other commercial interests

PostingID: 3048617759

A man called me about this about an hour after I posted it. While he was talking to me, he was browsing through my listings using my awesome search function and found 3 more things he bought from me.

Filing Cabinet—4 Drawer—$30 (Clarksville (Sango))

Date: 2012-06-10, 11:02AM EDT
Reply to: *your anonymous craigslist address will appear here*
This is an all black 4 drawer filing cabinet made by HON. This thing is incredible. The drawers all open and close and there is a ton of room to file documents in. I'm getting rid of this because we have no need to keep on filing paperwork. We're really not that important and pretty much everything that my wife has been filing away over the years can be thrown in the trash. I have a hard time believing that a Walmart receipt for a

10 pack of pencils needs to be saved for 15 years. I may just be naive though. Anyway, if you want this for my firm price of $30, then text or call me at 931-249-7016. If you're interested in some other great deals, search 7016.

- Location: Clarksville (Sango)
- it's NOT ok to contact this poster with services or other commercial interests

PostingID: 3068858954

Facebook sold this one for me to a friend. The best part was that he stopped by to drink a few beers with me before he took this off my hands.

Coffee Table—$50 (Clarksville (Sango))

Date: 2012-06-10, 9:14AM EDT

Reply to: *your anonymous craigslist address will appear here*

After the successful garage sale this weekend, I told my wife it would be a good idea for her to leave town for a few days to visit her sister. Now with her being gone, I will have no problem selling all of the stuff she doesn't want sold. I'm starting with the beautiful, solid wood, mission style coffee table. This thing is classy to say the least. The top has a few cosmetic issues and could someday use a nice refinishing, but other than that, this table is in great shape. You can obviously use this table to put your coffee on, but what isn't so obvious is the other uses for this beast. It works great as a foot rest and the shelf on the bottom can be used to store crap that your wife and kids don't want to put away. For the most part, the shelf keeps these items completely hidden. The table can also be used to put books or magazines on and pretty much any other item you can think of. This table is a very heavy duty table and will not fit in the trunk of your Ford Taurus . . . so plan ahead when you come to pick it up. As with everything I'm selling on Craigslist, the price is firm and the first person to show up to my house and give me $50 gets to take it home. Text or call me at 931-249-7016. If you're in the market for more awesome stuff at low prices, search "7016" to see all of my listings.

- Location: Clarksville (Sango)
- it's NOT ok to contact this poster with services or other commercial interests

PostingID: 3068716143

I didn't get a single call on this for over a week. I finally sold this to a very nice man who was about to undergo some chemotherapy the following day.

Twin Bed with Mattress—Solid Wood—$75 (Clarksville (Sango))

Date: 2012-06-18, 4:45PM EDT
Reply to: *your anonymous craigslist address will appear here*

This is the last of my beds that I am listing. This is a solid wood bed. It is not pink but rather has a white washed finish (the painfully pink room makes it look that color). This bed is in excellent condition and my daughter just got done lying to me again about how she has never had an "accident" in it. This thing sits low to the ground which will limit emergency room trips due to falling off the bed. As with all of my items, this bed comes from a smoke and flatulence free home. Once this is sold, my children will all be sleeping on the floor. They're really excited about that opportunity. $75 is my firm price and if you are interested, text or call me at 931-249-7016. Search "7016" to see my other listings.

- Location: Clarksville (Sango)
- it's NOT ok to contact this poster with services or other commercial interests

PostingID: 3077771073

*It took over a week before someone bought this. Finally, a very nice lady
and her two teenage daughters showed up to my house to pick this up. My
awesome neighbor, A.K., helped me load everything into their two trucks and
I was $750 richer.*

Bedroom Set—King Size—$750 (Clarksville (Sango))

Date: 2012-06-10, 9:17AM EDT
Reply to: *your anonymous craigslist address will appear here*

I'm probably jumping the gun a little with this listing, but I've had so
much fun selling stuff today that I'm just gonna list this right now. This is
a King Size Solid Wood Bedroom Set. It's spectacular!!! It is made of real
wood and besides a few minor cosmetic things, it's in great shape. It comes
with the bed frame, foot board, head board and mattress and box springs.
There are two dressers and one has a big mirror attached to the top so you
can look at yourself whenever you walk through your room. It also has two
matching night stands. All of the drawers open and close and you can put
stuff in them. Nothing illegal in the state of Tennessee has ever been done
in this bed and I have never had an "accident" in it. As with everything I'm
selling, this item comes from a smoke and flatulence free home. This was
purchased for way too much money about 6 or 7 years ago. It can be yours
for only $750. I'm keeping the pillows and the blankets however for a
future craigslisting. If you're interested in paying me my firm price for this
fine piece of furniture, then text or call me at 931-249-7016. You might
want to act quickly on this one before my wife pulls the listing (being that
we still have a while before we're moving). And while you're at it, check
out the other furniture I'm selling by searching 7016.

- Location: Clarksville (Sango)
- it's NOT ok to contact this poster with services or other
  commercial interests

PostingID: 3068719718

Somebody called me up within minutes of me posting the listing and offered me $45. A day later I got my asking price from someone who had some common sense and realized this was a good deal.

Benches and Baskets—Ikea—$50 (Clarksville (Sango))

Date: 2012-06-10, 10:08AM EDT
Reply to: *your anonymous craigslist address will appear here*

Here's another wonderful deal that is a result of my plan to get rid of everything I have while my wife is out of town for the week. This is an IKEA bench that comes with 3 little baskets (I think the baskets are IKEA as well). These benches and baskets are in excellent condition and are maybe a year old or so. We used them in our foyer for the kids to put their shoes under and to put whatever other crap they have in order for us to give the false impression that our house is actually clean and things are put where they go. The benches and baskets work great for this. If you're interested in this awesome deal, text or call me at 931-249-7016. My price is firm at $30 per bench/basket set or $50 for both sets. Search "7016" if you would like to see what else I'm selling.

- Location: Clarksville (Sango)
- it's NOT ok to contact this poster with services or other commercial interests

PostingID: 3068779041

Right after I posted this, a woman sent me an email saying that she could buy the same thing at Walmart for the same price I was asking. About 5 hours later all three were being carried out of my house and I had $100.

Book Shelf—$40 (Clarksville (Sango))

Date: 2012-06-10, 10:45AM EDT
Reply to: *your anonymous craigslist address will appear here*

I'm listing 3 books shelves in this one listing because I'm lazy. In the pictures, the shelves have books and other items on them . . . . these things are not included. So, 1 Book shelf is about 6' tall and I want $40 for it. The other two are about 3 feet tall (maybe a little taller . . . . I'm lazy and I don't feel like going up stairs to measure them). The small shelves are $30 a piece. I just did the math on my calculator app on the phone and all of that adds up to $100. These book shelves are in good condition and they are black with a wood grain. They're pretty heavy and they look awesome (that's why I bought them). If you interested in one or all of these things, then text or call me at 931-249-7016. My wife just left town for a few days so act quickly before she gets back and sees what I'm up to. The prices are firm as always and if you'd like to see the other items I'm selling, search "7016."

- Location: Clarksville (Sango)
- it's NOT ok to contact this poster with services or other commercial interests

PostingID: 3068833055

It took 4 days before somebody decided to buy this.

Filing Cabinet—4 Drawer—$30 (Clarksville (Sango))

Date: 2012-06-10, 11:02AM EDT
Reply to: *your anonymous craigslist address will appear here*

* * *UPDATE* * *The black filing cabinet sold almost instantly. This motivated me to sell the white one (which I wasn't planning on selling). So because I'm too lazy to come up with a new listing, the following listing applies. Just replace the word "black", with the word "white" throughout the listing. Also, you can see half of the filing cabinet in the picture. If you buy this by tomorrow, I will throw in the 5 gallon bucket that is pictured next to the black filing cabinet for free.* * *

This is an all black 4 drawer filing cabinet made by HON. This thing is incredible. The drawers all open and close and there is a ton of room to file documents in. I'm getting rid of this because we have no need to keep on filing paperwork. We're really not that important and pretty much everything that my wife has been filing away over the years can be thrown in the trash. I have a hard time believing that a Walmart receipt for a 10pack of pencils needs to be saved for 15 years. I may just be naive though. Anyway, if you want this for my firm price of $30, then text or call me at 931-249-7016. If you're interested in some other great deals, search 7016.

- Location: Clarksville (Sango)
- it's NOT ok to contact this poster with services or other commercial interests

PostingID: 3068858954

This was sold 3 hours after I listed it.

Computer Desk—$20 (Clarksville (Sango))

Date: 2012-06-10, 11:10AM EDT
Reply to: *your anonymous craigslist address will appear here*

This is in my opinion the best computer desk on the market. I feel this way because it has doors that close. These doors completely hide the mess that your wife and kids have in the computer desk because they can't just put things away. The reason the doors are closed in the picture is because it is a mess inside. If the doors were open in the picture and if there wasn't a mess in there, you would see a place for a monitor, a few shelves, and keyboard drawer that pulls in and out, and place for a desktop computer, and a bunch of storage space. If you like the all black wood grain coloring on this thing, then check out the matching bookshelves I'm selling by going here: http://clarksville.craigslist.org/fuo/3068833055.html If you're interested in this for my firm price of $20, then text or call me at 931-249-7016. Search "7016" to see the other items I'm selling.

- Location: Clarksville (Sango)
- it's NOT ok to contact this poster with services or other commercial interests

PostingID: 3068871359

Shortly after I posted this, a woman called me and asked me if I would take $30. I obviously declined that generous offer. She called me back an hour later and said she wanted it, but she didn't know if it would fit in the trunk of her Honda Civic. It is so obvious when people are the product of lower class inbreeding. Later on that day it sold for $35 to a normal person.

6 Foot Folding Table—$35 (Clarksville (Sango))

Date: 2012-06-10, 11:46AM EDT
Reply to: *your anonymous craigslist address will appear here*

This is a 6 Foot Folding Table. It is a table with legs that fold. It is in great condition. For those of you who graciously allowed me to borrow your folding tables for my garage sale this weekend . . . . do not worry . . . . this is my wife's table and yours is still in my garage and will not be sold on Craigslist. I will return them just as soon as my wife returns from her out of town trip and I have a vehicle large enough to move them. Additionally, if this table sells and my dining room table sells, I may need to borrow one of the folding tables for a little bit longer so we have something to eat on . . . . I'll keep people posted. Maybe I can just lease one of the folding tables by the day or something. I'm not really sure what I'm gonna do about chairs though. Anyway, if you're interested in buying this from me for $35 instead of for $80 at Walmart, text or call me at 931-249-7016. Search "7016" to see my other listings.

- Location: Clarksville (Sango)
- it's NOT ok to contact this poster with services or other commercial interests

PostingID: 3068932266

This was purchased by a friend of the woman who purchased my sewing machine. People love to talk about the great deals they find on Craigslist

Computer Chair—$10 (Clarksville (Sango))

Date: 2012-06-10, 12:32PM EDT
Reply to: *your anonymous craigslist address will appear here*

This is an all black computer chair. It is in excellent condition and it turns around in circles. My kids use this as a merry-go-round. I use it as a chair. My wife will be back by Thursday at which time she will surely pull this listing. Act fast . . . . text or call 931-249-7016. My price is firm. Search "7016" to see my other listings.

- Location: Clarksville (Sango)
- it's NOT ok to contact this poster with services or other commercial interests

PostingID: 3069015333

I wasn't sure whether or not to list this or take it to the dump. It sold the same day I listed it and saved me a trip to the landfill.

Dresser—Kids—$5 (Clarksville (Sango))

Date: 2012-06-11, 11:37AM EDT
Reply to: *your anonymous craigslist address will appear here*

I'm not really sure what this is, I just know that I want to sell it for $5. It looks like a dresser to me. My daughter uses it to put stuff in. It has a drawer on the top and and door on the bottom. It's about 4 feet tall and maybe 2 feet wide. It has pink handles. Whatever this is, it is in good condition and it will look awesome in your house. If you're interested, text or call me at 931-249-7016. My price is firm as always and if you search "7016", you can see the other things I'm selling.

- Location: Clarksville (Sango)
- it's NOT ok to contact this poster with services or other commercial interests

PostingID: 3070767308

This sold very quickly to an Army NCO who wanted it for her son. She said she thought that maybe I had made a mistake when I listed it for only $350. I told her I hadn't and she said she didn't need the lower bed. So she took everything else, I took $350 and then relisted the bottom bed for $75. I figured it was OK to break up a set in that case.

Loft Bunk Bed—Bedroom Set with Dresser and Desk—Solid Wood—$350 (Clarksville (Sango))

Date: 2012-06-12, 10:32AM EDT

Reply to: *your anonymous craigslist address will appear here*

I was originally planning on taking this with me on our upcoming move. I have just been having so much fun selling stuff while my wife is out of town that I figured I'd at least post this. I still have two days before she

returns from her trip . . . . that should be plenty of time for this to sell. This is an awesome solid wood Bunk Bed Bedroom Set. It has two twin sized matresses, a stand-alone dresser, a desk built into the bunk bed, shelves built into the side of the bunk bed and 4 drawers built into the bunk bed. This set is in excellent condition and I paid $1000 for it a few years ago. It can be yours for the non-negotiable price of $350. Prior to listing this, I had a meeting with my two daughters who sleep on this setup. They both assured me that they have never "wet" these beds. I can assure you without a doubt that they are both lying to me. However . . . the plastic cover thingys on the matresses have insured that no urine ever got onto the actual matresses. If you're interested in purchasing this fine bunk bed set from me, text or call me at 931-249-7016. If you would like to view the other listings I have, search "7016"

- Location: Clarksville (Sango)
- it's NOT ok to contact this poster with services or other commercial interests

PostingID: 3072875927

CHAPTER 5

SOME PICTURES

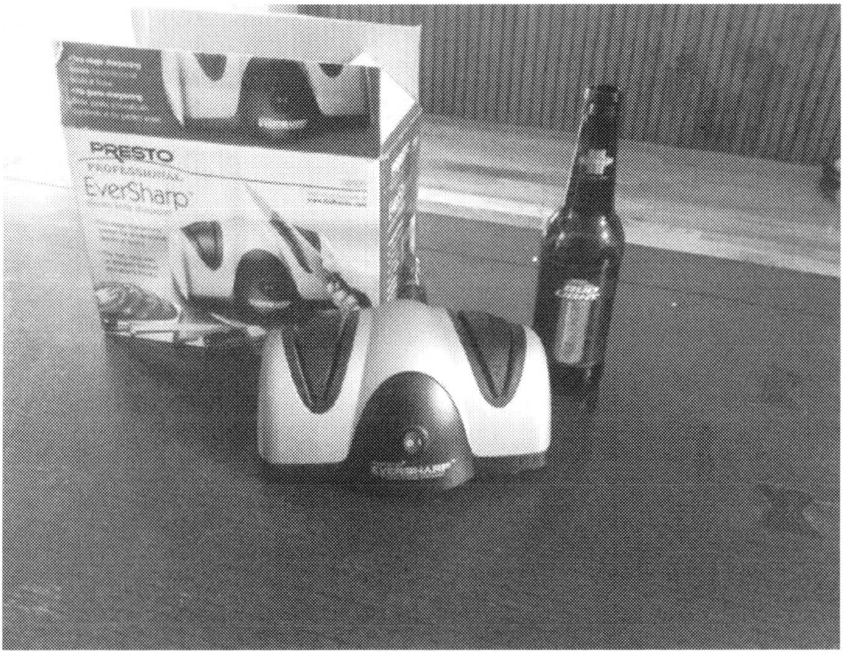
PRESTO
PROFESSIONAL
EverSharp

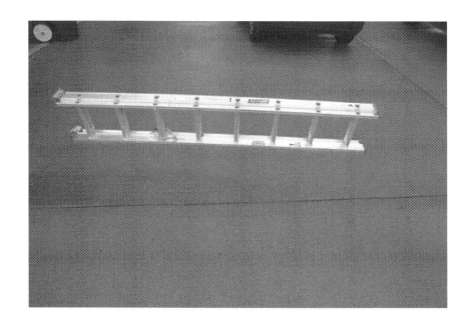

CHAPTER 6

YOUR LISTINGS

PHONE NUMBER

Always put your phone number in the advertisement. People are naturally afraid to post their phone number because they don't want to get unsolicited advertisements or random people calling them. I have never had this problem, and I have put my phone number in every one of my listings. From my experience, all phishing schemes on Craigslist come in the form of emails that are in response to your listing. In order to bypass this, post your phone number in the listing and be very careful when responding to emails. People who are interested in buying things on Craigslist want to be able to get instant responses. Emails are not the way to do this. By putting your phone number in the listing, people will contact you by phone as soon as they read the listing. I have actually been told by people who have bought my items that the main reason they contacted me and not somebody else was because I had put my phone number in the advertisement.

BE DESCRIPTIVE

Most listings on Craigslist simply state what the item is. Make your listing stand out by being descriptive. It only takes an extra minute to give measurements or to state what the item actually does. Simply typing out what the description on the "box" says about the item will give people an idea about what they are buying. If someone is looking for a sewing machine, they are more likely to buy one where the listing actually talks about the specific features of the sewing machine you're selling as opposed to a listing that just says "I'm selling this sewing machine." If you don't know much about the item, do a Google search and then copy and paste the item description straight off the internet. Spend the extra minute to make your listing actually say something useful.

USE SOME HUMOR

As you have seen in my listings, I like to use humor. I started doing this just to amuse myself, but I found that humor made my listings stand out. I have had many people tell me that the only reason they purchased an item from me was because of the strange description of it. To me, humor is a great tool to catch a prospective buyer's attention. Because of the humor in my ads, my listings started gaining a following of people in the local area who would search for them just to read the next stupid thing I was about to write. Eventually, people who never had any intention of buying my items would find an item they liked and then come buy it from me.

COMPARE PRICES IN YOUR DESCRIPTION

Let people know how much the same item would cost them new and used. You've already done your research, so share it. If you can buy the same thing you're selling online for $100 new and for $75 used, then tell people that. Let them know that they are getting away like thieves by buying it from you for $65.

DON'T "BREAK UP" A SET

I have had a lot of people call me about listings I've posted, asking me if I would be willing to sell them just a part or piece of what I've listed. For example, somebody once called me about a bedroom set I was selling and asked if I would sell just the mattress and the frame. I would highly recommend that you never break something up that is part of set. It will be so much harder to sell all the parts and pieces individually. Just be patient and eventually somebody will call you and want the complete item.

BE CAREFUL ABOUT HOLDING AN ITEM
FOR A POTENTIAL BUYER

Most Craigslist buyers are flakes. Be very clear in your listing that you will not hold an item for someone. If they want something that you are selling, then they better race to your house to get it. If you tell someone that you'll "hold" the item for them, I have found that about half of the time they'll never show up. Make people race to get what you're selling. I have made a few exceptions to this, but for the most part, the first person who shows up to my house and gives me the money gets the item.

MAKE SURE YOU POST A PICTURE, BUT REMEMBER THAT IT'S JUST A PICTURE

It takes a few seconds to take a picture of the item you're selling and then upload it into your listing. I am amazed at how many listings I have seen that have no pictures. Nobody is going to even contact you about your dining room table if you don't at least give them a picture of it. With that being said, take minimal time on taking pictures. People know what it is that you're selling by the description already, so don't set up a professional photo studio. Just take a picture and who really cares what is in the background. Nobody is going to be concerned with the empty beer can next to the Cuisinart you're selling. In fact, I have had people call me, inquiring about items they saw in the background of a picture in my listings. Prospective buyers just need an idea of what your item looks like so they can make the decision of whether or not they want to come to your house to see it in person.

UTILIZE A SEARCH FEATURE

If you have multiple listings on Craigslist, you should utilize some sort of search feature. It took me about a week before I realized that Craigslist had no way for people to search for all the items that I was listing. I found that the only way for a person to see everything I was selling was if I inserted a keyword for which people could search. Since I always put my phone number in all of my listings, I started writing into the end of each listing for people to search the last four digits of my phone number to see the other items that I was selling. I have been amazed at how many people have purchased multiple items because they used the search feature I built into my ads. I have also had many people tell me that they bought an item from me because they read a completely different listing and found it to be funny. They started reading all of my listings and soon found something they wanted to buy.

SMOKE-FREE HOME

If you're not a smoker, then let people know it by saying so in your listing. Nobody wants to come all the way out to your house to buy a chair and then when they get there find that it smells like smoke. For items that are made of cloth or some type of fabric, state in the ad that the item comes from a smoke-free home. On the other side of that, if you are a smoker, you're probably going to want to do a bang-up job of hiding the stench in the item you're selling.

RENEW YOUR LISTINGS

Every three days, Craigslist allows you to "renew" your listing. When a person uses Craigslist to search for a particular item, the item that was most recently posted will be at the top of the list that they see. When you initially post your listing, your item will be at the top and then over time, it will work its way down to the bottom. In order to keep your listing as close to the top as possible, it is important to renew it every three days. By doing this, your listing will be the first item that is seen by a prospective buyer.

CHAPTER 7

KIDS STUFF

I am a man of my word and I gave my girls $15.

Wooden Train Set & Train Table—$50 (Clarksville (Sango))

Date: 2012-05-13, 7:39PM EDT
Reply to: *your anonymous craigslist address will appear here*

I'm selling this awesome Solid Wood Train Table that I personally built along with this wooden train track set and all of these cool trains and the rest of the stuff you see on the train table in the pictures. If you were to go out and buy these items on your own, you'd spend millions . . . or maybe even a couple of hundred dollars. Everything is in real good condition and I've promised each of my 3 daughters 10% of the profits. If you're not good at math, that's 30% of $50. I'm not real good at math so after I post this ad, I'll go figure that one out on a calculator. This is probably one of the better deals you'll ever find . . . and as a side note, this stuff comes from a smoke free home. The $50 asking price is firm (unless you want to pay more). Call or text me at 931-249-7016. For a limited time only, if you call within 30 minutes of reading this, I'll help you load everything in your vehicle.

- Location: Clarksville (Sango)
- it's NOT ok to contact this poster with services or other commercial interests

PostingID: 3013656709

This one sold within 2 days of listing it.

Play Kitchen—$10 (Clarksville (Sango))

Date: 2012-05-18, 12:13AM EDT
Reply to: *your anonymous craigslist address will appear here*

I'm selling one of the better play kitchens that I've ever seen . . . . and I'm selling it for only $10. If you were to buy this thing brand new, you'd pay well over $10. This one however, looks almost exactly like it's new . . . yet it costs only $10. Let me do the math for you: you could pay well over ten bucks for this thing or you could pay exactly ten bucks for it . . . and it would look exactly like the one that you paid well over ten bucks for. This is a no-brainer!!! Now that I'm thinking about it, I might just buy this from myself and then sell it to you for $20 tomorrow. You better act fast before I do that! Call or text me at 931-249-7016. The price is firm and since I'm liquidating all of my assets (starting with my kid's toys), they aren't around for long. If you buy this on a day of the week that ends in a "Y", I'll throw in a free CD-R that is only partially scratched.

- Location: Clarksville (Sango)
- it's NOT ok to contact this poster with services or other commercial interests

PostingID: 3018252322

For over two weeks, nobody called on this, and then finally somebody saw it and gladly paid my asking price.

Fisher Price Dollhouse with Dolls & Accessories—$40 (Clarksville (Sango))

Date: 2012-05-25, 11:40PM EDT
Reply to: *your anonymous craigslist address will appear here*

Here's another great deal coming from my master plan to sell everything I own for dirt cheap prices. This is a Fisher Price Dollhouse with a big bin full of dolls and dollhouse accessories. I believe this is one of Fisher Price's "Loving Family" dollhouse sets . . . . and if thats the case, my wife is gonna be raging mad when she sees that I'm selling it for a fraction of the price she paid for it. Everything looks to be in good condition to me. The dolls and accessories are built to last. You can step on these things and your foot is the only thing that gets damaged. It hurts really bad to do this and it results in a lot of yelling on my part, yet the dolls and accessories don't make a sound. They just lay there on the floor . . . exactly in the spot I told my daughters not to put them. I expect this to sell fast, which means I've probably told my kids to stop leaving these toys on the floor for the last time. The price is firm and the first person to pay me the money gets this "house of joy." Call or text me at 931-249-7016. And if you're looking for more awesome stuff to buy, search "7016" in Craigslist. More stuff is being listed everyday . . . until it's all gone.

- Location: Clarksville (Sango)
- it's NOT ok to contact this poster with services or other commercial interests

PostingID: 3021209928

These were gone within 8 hours of listing them.

Toy Box—$10 (Clarksville (Sango))

Date: 2012-06-11, 12:32PM EDT
Reply to: *your anonymous craigslist address will appear here*

I'm selling two wooden toy boxes for $10 a piece. The toy boxes are 29 inches long, 14 inches deep, and 19 inches tall. These are in excellent condition and they work really well for storing lots of toys. You can even stuff a small child inside one of these things . . . they truly are marvelous toy boxes. If you're interested in buying one or both of these, text or call me at 931-249-7016. My price is firm and if you'd like to buy both and can't do the math on your own . . . you can get both for $20 . . . not $15. Search "7016" to see what else I'm selling.

- Location: Clarksville (Sango)
- it's NOT ok to contact this poster with services or other commercial interests

PostingID: 3070908706

Nothing Yet

Painting Easel—Kids—2 of them—$20 (Clarksville (Sango))

Date: 2012-06-10, 11:34AM EDT
Reply to: *your anonymous craigslist address will appear here*

I'm selling 2 kids painting easels. One of them is used but is in great condition and the other is brand new and still in the wrapper (made by IKEA). We have a problem in my house with buying stuff that we plan to use but just put in the garage for up to 10 years without ever opening it (by "we", I'm not referring to myself). The madness is about to stop

and you can be a part of my liquidation process by purchasing both of these for the low cost of $20. I'm also including a brand new, never been opened, I don't know why we have it, roll of IKEA easel paper. If you're interested in this stellar deal, text or call me at 931-249-7016. My price is firm and if you want more goodies that I'm selling, search "7016"

- Location: Clarksville (Sango)
- it's NOT ok to contact this poster with services or other commercial interests

PostingID: 3068911967

This was another rare item that I delivered. A man met me at the parking lot for swim lessons when I dropped my daughters off.

Car Seat—Alpha Omega—$10 (Clarksville (Sango))

Date: 2012-06-11, 11:03AM EDT
Reply to: *your anonymous craigslist address will appear here*

Here's the latest in my selling spree. I'm selling this Alpha Omega Car Seat for only $10. If you didn't know, "Alpha Omega" is French for "Super Safe." This is pretty much the mercedes benz of car seats. Thanks to this baby, I have 4 daughters who are alive and well and who are continuing to cost me lots of money. This car seat is in excellent condition. My price is firm and if you're interested in spending $10 instead of well over $100 for a car seat, text or call me at 931-249-7016. While you're at it, search "7016" to see the other awesome stuff I'm selling.

- Location: Clarksville (Sango)
- it's NOT ok to contact this poster with services or other commercial interests

PostingID: 3070686093

I had probably 10 people call me about this and claim they were coming to get it. Then about 5 days after I listed it a guy bought so he could hang his racing bike up on it.

Clothes Rack Hanger Up Thingy—$5 (Clarksville (Sango))

Date: 2012-06-11, 12:39PM EDT
Reply to: *your anonymous craigslist address will appear here*

This is a thing that you hang clothes up on or whatever other item you want to put on a clothes hanger and hang up. It is 3feet wide and 4feet tall and about a foot deep. My daughters used it to hang up all of their dress-up clothes. But I'm pretty sure it can be used to hang up most anything. It is all black (which is cool) and it is a great conversation piece during gatherings at the house. If you are interested in purchasing this for my firm price of $5, then text or call me at 931-249-7016. You can also search "7016" to see the other items I'm selling.

- Location: Clarksville (Sango)
- it's NOT ok to contact this poster with services or other commercial interests

PostingID: 3070926962

I sold one of these on the same day I listed it and then I had to wait almost 3 weeks before someone called about the other one.

Graco Booster Seat—$5 (Clarksville (Sango))

Date: 2012-06-11, 3:01PM EDT
Reply to: *your anonymous craigslist address will appear here*

I have 2 Graco Booster Seats to sell for $5 a piece. These seats are in good condition and are about 3 years old. They come with dual cup holders so your kids can double-fist NyQuil while you drive in peace and quiet. My price is firm . . . . and just to explain what that means (since there has been

some confusion lately with the items I've been listing) . . . . I will accept no less than $5 for a seat. If you want both seats, a quantity discount is not going to be offered. 5+5 =10. It does not equal $7.50. So if you are interested, text or call me at 931-249-7016. Search "7016" to see my other listings.

- Location: Clarksville (Sango)
- it's NOT ok to contact this poster with services or other commercial interests

PostingID: 3071293669

This sold almost instantly.

Toy Rack with lots of bins—$15 (Clarksville (Sango))

Date: 2012-06-01, 1:30PM EDT
Reply to: *your anonymous craigslist address will appear here*

Last night I sold my 7 year-old daughters dresser because it seemed extravagent for her to have a dresser. So in an act of defiance, she moved this toy rack with 14 bins into her room (it was already empty because I sold most of the toys a week ago). She is now using this thing as a dresser and is unaware that it will be gone by the end of the day. This rack is pretty awesome if I don't say so myself. It appears to be made of some sort of wood and it has 4 racks and 14 bins to put stuff in. Right now it is being used for clothes and none of the pictured clothes are for sale at the moment. If you want this for the low price of $15 then text or call me at 931-249-7016. Everything in my house is being sold because we're moving far away in the near future. So if you're interested in more of my items, then text or call 931-249-7016.

- Location: Clarksville (Sango)
- it's NOT ok to contact this poster with services or other commercial interests

PostingID: 3051111147

These sold real quick to a couple who drove up from Nashville to get them. They also bought two lamps from me that I hadn't even listed yet.

Toy Box—Wooden—$10 (Clarksville (Sango))

Date: 2012-06-12, 10:08AM EDT
Reply to: *your anonymous craigslist address will appear here*

I decided to sell two more toy boxes when I woke up this morning. These boxes are in great shape and I'm selling them for $10 a piece. They are

3 ft long X 20 inches tall X 16 inches deep. They have wheels which makes them super easy to move around the house or for the kids to pretend they're on a bobsled team. If you're interested in these, text or call me at 931-249-7016. When you text me, let me know at least 30 minutes in advance of the time you're coming over so I can get the toys removed from the boxes. Search "7016" to see more of my listings.

- Location: Clarksville (Sango)
- it's NOT ok to contact this poster with services or other commercial interests

PostingID: 3072827835

CHAPTER 8

OTHER STUFF WORTH NOTING

USE SOCIAL NETWORKING

You probably have a lot of friends, or perhaps your wife has a lot of friends, who are interested in your crap. You just don't know it yet. Post your listings on your Facebook page and you will greatly increase your chances of selling your items as quickly as possible.

GARAGE SALES

Craigslist is an awesome place to list your garage / moving sales. I would go as far as saying that you're an absolute bonehead if you don't list your garage sale on Craigslist. I had two garage sales within a two-month period and they were both quite successful.

My advice would be to always post a map of the location of your house, and then briefly list the type of items that you are selling. There are "professional" garage sale peeps who live for weekend garage sales. They search out these things online and then show up about 30 minutes before they start so they can grab the best stuff and then resell it. From my experience these people usually wear jean shorts that are too small for them and they have the personality of a brick. But who really cares . . . they're buying your crap because they think it's precious.

A lot of garage sale people like to have signs posted along their route of travel. I believe that is pointless. In this day and age, if you can't find an address with your GPS or with Mapquest, then you don't deserve to walk out your front door.

My garage sales worked out great for me. I obviously hate haggling, so I set all of my prices as "non-negotiable" and I sold virtually everything I had. So the moral of this story is that you should definitely use Craigslist to advertise your garage sale and set your prices as "firm" unless you just like getting nickel-and-dimed to death by people wearing very small jean shorts (aka jorts).

BE PREPARED TO WITNESS SOME DUMB STUFF

I found that by following my little rules I set up for selling my stuff, I was able to weed out the large majority of "special people" prior to them coming to my house to pay for and pick up an item. Probably 95% of my interactions with buyers were nothing short of pleasant. With that being said, "you can't stop stupid." No matter what you do, eventually you're going to run into "that guy" and the only thing you can do is have a good sense of humor.

You very well may find yourself face to face with a man who shows up to your house to pick up a 5 foot bookshelf with the intentions of cramming it into the trunk of his Ford Escort. In spite of the fact that your listing stated all of the dimensions and you actually spoke with him on the phone and told him how big it was, he will still show up with a half-baked plan of getting the bookshelf home. Even after he makes the visual assessment with the bookshelf standing right next to the car, this guy will not be prevented from trying to get it in the trunk. There is nothing you can say to him to convince him that without the use of a chainsaw, the bookshelf will not fit. He will say brilliant things like, "I can't believe how big this bookshelf is." You can respond to him by telling him that you think it might be five feet tall and three feet wide. It really doesn't matter what you say though because this man is driven by a motivation that evades all common sense. Sarcasm is completely lost on him and he probably won't hear a word you're saying because he is too busy attempting the impossible: forcing something that is 15 square-feet in size into a six square-foot trunk. Eventually, he will realize that he needs to go borrow a friend's truck and an hour or two later, he'll get his bookshelf home.

My point is that my "rules" that I use for listing items do a great job of vetting potential buyers who are not serious about paying my asking price. The problem is that there are a few people who are very serious about paying you what you're asking, but who just aren't the brightest individuals. So keep a sense of humor and be prepared to be a witness to evolution in reverse.

BE SAFE

You never really know who it is that you've been texting or talking to about buying your item that you listed on Craigslist. My advice is to use common sense. I always allow people to come to my house to pick up the item they're buying, but I never give them my address until they are on their way to my house. I know that I can't be sure that they're on their way, but I don't feel the need to just give out my address the first time they ask. If I'm not home, I will not set up a time for them to pick up the item with only my wife being at home. I don't think there is any fool proof way to be safe, but you can definitely use some common sense to make things as safe as possible. Some people feel that it is safer to meet the buyer at a public place, but I don't like bringing an item to anyone or meeting them anywhere if it's out of my way, especially if the item they are buying is of little value. To me, it makes no sense to drive to Walmart to meet up with someone just so they can give me $5 for a lamp. I might as well just throw the lamp in the trash and save my gas and time.

CHAPTER 9

OTHER STUFF THAT'S FUN TO SELL

Another sale due to Facebook. In my opinion, the guy who bought this most likely bought it because he idolizes me. You can admit it, Carl.

Jackson Titanium Shovel—$10 (Clarksville (Sango))

Date: 2012-05-14, 10:37PM EDT
Reply to: *your anonymous craigslist address will appear here*

I'm selling this rugged Jackson Titanium Shovel with a fiberglass handle. This shovel is indestructable!!! The main reason I'm selling this is because when I woke up this morning I decided that I don't ever want to dig again . . . for the rest of my life. But then when I walk into the garage and see Jackson standing there, I have the uncontrollable urge to go dig a hole. Our backyard looks terrible now and my wife is really upset. This shovel is ruining my life . . . but I love it anyway. $10 is my firm price. The first person to hand me the money gets the shovel. Call or text 931-249-7016. The shovel is dirty, but other than that it is in excellent condition.

- Location: Clarksville (Sango)
- it's NOT ok to contact this poster with services or other commercial interests

PostingID: 3016012361

Facebook, again.

Luggage Rack and Cargo Bag—Hitch Mounted—$75 (Clarksville (Sango))

Date: 2012-05-15, 10:12AM EDT
Reply to: *your anonymous craigslist address will appear here*

This is the Pro Series 63153 Black 60" x 24" Hitch Mounted Cargo Carrier and the Rola 59102 Expandable Hitch Tray Cargo Bag. I purchased them together from Amazon in december for $190 plus shipping. They were used on a road trip from TN to WA in December and worked great. The bag is quite impressive. Completely water proof and very rugged. Plus they look cool. I was amazed at the number of beautiful women who went out of their way to compliment me on this setup. The Rack weighs about 60 pounds and is rated for a 500 pound load . . . plus you don't even know it's behind you and it does not affect your gas mileage. I absolutely love these but my current situation dictates that I must sell these along with everything else I own. That's precisely why I'm almost giving them away. People have been contacting my quickly on Items i've posted so far. So act fast and text or call 931-249-7016. The price is "firm" and the first person who gives me the money gets the merchandise. Act now and I'll throw in a free can of partially used acetone that is in my garage!!! My wife no longer allows me to use the acetone after I ruined a table while conducting an experiment.

- Location: Clarksville (Sango)
- it's NOT ok to contact this poster with services or other commercial interests

PostingID: 3016569590

Not a single person called me on this for almost two weeks. Then one day, someone all the way across the state saw this listing and had a family member who lived close by come and purchase it.

Shop Vac Wet/Dry 20Gal 6.5HP—$75 (Clarksville (Sango))

Date: 2012-05-17, 7:33AM EDT
Reply to: *your anonymous craigslist address will appear here*

Here's a great deal on a used Shop Vac. This same thing sells for $170 at lowes. Even though this is used, I highly doubt a new one sucks any harder than this one. I love this shop vac so much! I would keep it for the rest of my life, but sadly, I'm moving to a country that frowns upon 110v equipment. So this guy is staying behind. $75 is my firm price, unless of course you feel the need to pay me more. I'm obviously making a terrible decision by giving this away for such a cheap price, but I've spent a large part of my adult life making terrible decisions. So it's really no big deal. Call or text me at 931-249-7016. The first person who hands me $75 gets this . . . . so act fast! If you buy this within 1 hour of viewing this listing, I'll throw in a free gallon (or what's left of the gallon) of pink paint I have left over from my daughter's room.

- Location: Clarksville (Sango)
- it's NOT ok to contact this poster with services or other commercial interests

PostingID: 3015991372

A friend saw this on Facebook and called a friend of his who was in the market for this exact rower. It was sold within 4 hours of posting the listing.

Rowing Machine—Concept 2—Model D PM3—$700 (Clarksville (Sango))

Date: 2012-05-24, 8:42PM EDT
Reply to: *your anonymous craigslist address will appear here*

Do you need a subtle way to tell that special someone in your life that they are fat and lazy? Or perhaps you're fat and lazy. Here is the answer you've been waiting for. This is a barely been used, in perfect condition, Concept 2 Model D Rowing Machine. This rower is amazing!!! It's what all of the professional athletes use (I have no way of backing up that claim). I do know for sure that you will find this fine piece of equipment at most of the high-end gyms. Another great thing about this rower is that it looks nice just sitting in your garage not being used. It wreaks of class. I would not be surprised to find this in a person's living room because of it's furniture-like appeal. I don't know very much about this rower because I've never used it (it belongs to my wife and she's unaware of it being sold on Craigslist). I do know that it has a little computer screen and an internal computer that allows you to choose workouts and then it tells you how fast you row a certain distance. It also has a seat, a place to put your feet and a rower-handle-thing that you pull. It also folds up to save space!! I think NASA may have invented some of these features. We've only owned this for a few months and we bought it on Amazon for $900.00 plus around $100.00 shipping. That comes to almost exactly $1000.00. You can still buy it on Amazon right now for $900.00 plus $100.00 shipping. Or you can buy it on ebay right now for $725.00 plus $125.00 shipping. That comes to almost exactly $850.00. Or if you're smart, you can buy it from me for $700.00 and $5.00 in gas to pick it up. I'm throwing a lot of numbers around right now, so I'm not gonna try to calculate the savings for you . . . but you can save a lot by buying this from me. Plus, unlike Amazon and eBay, I'm throwing in a free coozy. It is blue and it says "Middle Tennessee Oral & Implant Surgery, PLLC" on it. This is an awesome coozy and it will keep your beer ice cold for you while you row on your new rower. Call or text me at 931-249-7016 if you're interested. I'm not budging on the price and don't expect me to take your word about how you're showing up this evening to pick it up. The first person who shows up and gives me $700 gets to take this home.

- Location: Clarksville (Sango)
- it's NOT ok to contact this poster with services or other commercial interests

PostingID: 3036450515

It took over 3 weeks before somebody decided that this was a good deal. I met him at a gas station by my house and then took his $20 and bought some beer.

Poker Chip Set—600 Piece—$20 (Clarksville (Sango))

Date: 2012-05-25, 11:40PM EDT
Reply to: *your anonymous craigslist address will appear here*

I'm selling everything I own because I'm moving to a foreign land with my wife and kids. All prices are non-negotiable (unless you wanna pay me more than I'm asking). Basically . . . I'm dumping my belongings off for dirt cheap prices and I don't feel like wasting time haggling. Usually when I list an item I get at least 5 text messages within the first hour . . . . I will not promise an item to anyone. If you're the first person to show up to my house . . . and if you pay me the money I'm asking . . . . then you get the item. This is a 600 piece clay poker chip set. I have won approximately $500 dollars in illegal overseas poker games with these chips. They work great. They come with the case and 5 dice, a dealer chip and here's the kicker: two sets of used cards . . . . don't pass up on this deal!!!! Contact me within 5 minutes of reading this ad and I'll throw in two (2) poker books. Call or text 931-249-7016

- Location: Clarksville (Sango)
- it's NOT ok to contact this poster with services or other commercial interests

PostingID: 3003873838

This one took awhile. Almost 3 weeks before I got anyone to call on it.

Extension Ladder 16ft—$65 (Clarksville (Sango))

Date: 2012-05-28, 4:09PM EDT
Reply to: *your anonymous craigslist address will appear here*

This is a used 16' Extension Ladder made by Louisville, Model # L-2323-16. The ladder is in excellent condition, as I've only used it 3 or 4 times. It has a few paint stains and some cobwebs (the cobwebs will wipe off). You can buy this new for anywhere between $140 and $220. This ladder is obviously not new, but it works just like a new ladder. You can climb up it or down it. It truly is an amazing ladder. I absolutely love this ladder and it breaks my heart to have to sell it. Every time I look at it I feel the need to climb it, but I'm just too lazy to pull it out of the garage. The only reason I'm parting with this "natural wonder" is because my family and I are moving out of the country and we can't take this with us. My selling price is firm and I will not hold this item for you. So what this means to you is that the first person who shows up to my house and gives me $65 gets to take this ladder home. I've been selling off almost everything in my house at these rock bottom prices and they've been going quick. This will be gone within an hour from now . . . so act fast. Call or text 931-249-7016. Additionally, as you can tell from the first picture, this ladder sometimes appears to be hovering about a foot off the ground . . . . it is an amazing ladder!!

- Location: Clarksville (Sango)
- it's NOT ok to contact this poster with services or other commercial interests

PostingID: 3015318492

Because I was selling these in the middle of the summer, I had to set the price a little low. It took about 2 weeks before anyone called me about them, and all 3 sold to the same person.

Down Comforter (3 of them) Home Classics—$60 (Clarksville (Sango))

Date: 2012-05-28, 4:09PM EDT
Reply to: *your anonymous craigslist address will appear here*

This might be the best bargain I've got going yet!!!! I'm selling 3 . . . . thats right!!! 3!!! Home Classics Down Comforters. They are used, but in excellent condition and they come with the original plastic cases. And the cases have the price tags on the back. Since they look new, this is a perfect way to pretend to be giving someone a really expensive brand new gift. According to the price tags on these, my wife had the audacity to pay $399.97 for these!!! I'm selling all 3 for $60. The place that I'm forcing my family to move to has temperatures that make it quite unnecessary for down comforters . . . so these aren't going with us. All 3 of these are for a twin sized bed. Another option for you, if you're not into passing off things as expensive gifts, is to buy these, keep one, and then sell the other two for a hundred bucks a piece. If you did that, you would technically be getting paid $140 to take these. So think about it . . . . if you're interested text or call me at 931-249-7016. Winter is just around the corner and these comforters will keep you warm. And if you're as worried about this upcoming winter as I am, check out this deal I posted the other day: http://clarksville.craigslist.org/for/3018275038.html My asking price of $60 is non-negotable . . . so act fast before I raise the price. *   *   *JUST IN CASE YOU WANT A KING SIZE HOME CLASSICS DOWN ALTERNATIVE COMFORTER THAT LOOKS ALMOST EXACTLY LIKE IT'S NEW, I'LL THROW MY WIFE'S IN FOR AN ADDITIONAL $40* *   * I just did the math on that one using the "calculator" application in windows and that would bring the total for all 4 comforters to $100.

- Location: Clarksville (Sango)
- it's NOT ok to contact this poster with services or other commercial interests

PostingID: 3021269994

I made $397 selling stuff that was absolutely worthless to me. My daughters made $48 from their lemonade and cookie sales.

Everything's $1 Garage / Moving Sale—June 8 & 9—$1 (Clarksville (Sango))

Date: 2012-05-30, 6:27PM EDT
Reply to: *your anonymous craigslist address will appear here*

I will be hosting a no-haggle garage sale on the mornings of Friday, June 8 and Saturday, June 9. This is gonna be super fun! The garage sale will start at 7am (no showing up early. If you show up before 7:50, you will be forced to go to the back of the line) and go until noon on both days. On Friday the 8th, everything will be $1 and on Saturday the 9th, everything will be 50 cents. It doesn't matter what the item is, as long as I'm selling it the price is fixed at a buck on Friday and fitty cent on Saturday. For $1, you could very likely come away with a brand-new-never-been-used-I-don't-know-why we purchased-it-for-30-bucks-snow shovel. Or for $1 you could come home with a dried umbilical cord thing that my wife saved from one of our kids. You just never know. I don't want to negotiate, so you're gonna hafta give me the entire $1 for the umbilical cord thingy . . . if you do try talking me down on the price, security will escort you off of the premises. I'll be selling a lot of little girls clothes and probably some tools and pretty much everything in my house that I haven't already sold on Craigslist. Additionally, my small children will be selling lemonade and cookies during the garage sale in order to raise money for me to buy beer in the afternoon. I've also heard them mention that they may be selling live toads. Should be a lot of fun. I live about 5 minutes off exit 11. My address is 1224 Voyage Ct, Adams, TN 37010. I have attached a picture of a map to my house.

North is up. Additionally, I have included a picture of me wearing a 3 wolf-moon shirt (just so you realize how serious this garage sale is). If you have any questions, text or call 931-249-7016. And while you're waiting for this awesome garage sale to kick off, check out the rest of the items I'm selling on Craigslist by searching "7016". As a side note: I have had a serious problem with selling things on Craigslist that are in and around my house. Pretty much if I see something that isn't moving, I take a picture of it and sell it on here. So, as a safety precaution, when you are in my yard looking at items, try not to stay in one position for more than 10 seconds . . . just keep moving. I'd hate to accidentally list you on Craigslist.

- • Location: Clarksville (Sango)
- • it's NOT ok to contact this poster with services or other commercial interests

PostingID: 3047582557

These sold about 3 days after I listed them. I felt kind of bad because an elderly woman was planning on coming to get them later in the week after her hair appointment. She was really disappointed when she called me and found out they were gone.

House Plants—12 of them—$25 (Clarksville (Sango))

Date: 2012-05-31, 11:50AM EDT
Reply to: *your anonymous craigslist address will appear here*

I am selling 12 of my wife's house plants that have been bothering me lately. These are really nice plants that my wife paid way too much money for at Lowes. Some of them look like trees. There are 12 plants that I'm selling and some of them come with really pretty containers and they have those expensive plastic things on the bottom of the bowls that keeps water from getting all over the floor. One of the really cool things about these plants is that they are all of the rare variety of plants that actually has the ability to create oxygen as a result of a thing called photosynthesis. I don't want to get all scientific on you, but basically what happens is that in the morning, after the moon has turned into the sun, the plants use the sunlight, carbon dioxide and water to create oxygen. The fact that these plants have been creating oxygen over the past year is probably one of the main reasons why my wife and kids are alive and breathing today. $25 is a non-negotiable price and if you're interested is these pretty green things, then text or call me at 931-249-7016.

- Location: Clarksville (Sango)
- it's NOT ok to contact this poster with services or other commercial interests

PostingID: 3048767040

It took about a week before somebody called on this. He showed up about 20 minutes later and I was 10 bucks richer and minus a leaf blower.

Leaf Blower—Weed Eater 2560—$10 (Clarksville (Sango))

Date: 2012-05-31, 9:49AM EDT
Reply to: *your anonymous craigslist address will appear here*

If you're one of those people that does a lot of your shopping here on Craigslist, then you most definitely have purchased some items that suck. Here is your opportunity to get out of that rut and buy something that blows. This is the Weed Eater Groundskeeper Plus (Model 2560). This baby is pristine!!! It is a 120V, 60hz, 85amp leaf blower. But it doesn't just blow leaves. This thing has the power to blow really small pieces of gravel across your driveway in 6-inch increments. Truly amazing!! This is powered by electricity (just plug an extension cord into the back and off you go. And assuming that you care about the environment and are a "green" person . . . . then this is the leaf blower you want. It isn't necessarily powered in environmentally friendly ways, but it is bright green in color. $10 is my firm price for this blowing-beast. Text or call 931-249-7016 and if you want more of my crap, search "7016" to see what I have listed.

- Location: Clarksville (Sango)
- it's NOT ok to contact this poster with services or other commercial interests

PostingID: 3048513623

It only took 3 days to find somebody who wanted to come pick these up for 10 bucks.

Dishes—A whole bunch of them—$10 (Clarksville (Sango))

Date: 2012-06-01, 12:19PM EDT
Reply to: *your anonymous craigslist address will appear here*

In order to become a "greener" person, I have decided to force my family to start recycling everything. Because of this, we're switching over to a "paper dishes" inventory. This brilliant move is going to allow the first lucky person who shows up to my house to walk away with these beautiful dishes for only $10. Some of these dishes are made by Gibson and some are made by Pier 1 and some are made by someone else. All of these dishes are clean, except for I put them on the floor so I could take a picture of them. They were on the floor for a little over 5-seconds so the 5-second rule does not technically apply. However, I personally would have no problem eating off of these without washing them . . . . this decision is going to come down to your personal beliefs on germs and your assessment of the cleanliness of my floors. For the most part these dishes are in great shape. If you're interested, text or call me at 931-249-7016. My price is firm and the first person to give me 10 bucks gets the dishes. Search 7016 if you'd like to see what other things I'm pretty much giving away.

- Location: Clarksville (Sango)
- it's NOT ok to contact this poster with services or other commercial interests

PostingID: 305093835

A really cool older woman called me about these. She said she was a little worried about showing up to someone's house late at night so she brought along her friend who was about the same age. I helped the two ladies load their new plant urns up into the truck and I had 25 bucks to go buy beer with.

Plant Urn—Large—2 of them—Super Cool—$25 (Clarksville (Sango))

Date: 2012-06-01, 1:19PM EDT
Reply to: *your anonymous craigslist address will appear here*

I'm selling 2 extremely classy looking plant urns that belong to my wife. These things are probably 2 ft tall. They're in good shape and I've had so many compliments on these that I've stopped answering my doorbell. People who are just driving through the neighborhood will actually stop and park in front of my house and then ring the doorbell just to tell me how nice these urns look (most of these gawkers are extremely attractive women). You would probably pay at least $50 apiece for urns like these . . . but not from me you won't. $25 is all I want and to sweeten this deal even more, I'm including a bunch of dirt and two trees that are already in the urns and well established. This will come as a surprise to you, but I am not a certified treeologist. With that as a disclaimer I would say that these trees are probably fir trees. If you're interested in purchasing these for my firm price of 25 bucks, then text or call me at 931-249-7016. I'm selling everything in my house so check out my other listings by searching 7016.

- Location: Clarksville (Sango)
- it's NOT ok to contact this poster with services or other commercial interests

PostingID: 3051082583

I actually split these up and sold them for a quarter each in my garage sale and doubled my profit.

Diet Coke—8 Pack—$1 (Clarksville (Sango))

Date: 2012-06-07, 10:34AM EDT
Reply to: *your anonymous craigslist address will appear here*

I'm selling 8, Ice Cold Diet Cokes for a buck. These have been in my fridge for 5 days now and I don't like how they take up space that could be used for beer. In my opinion Diet Coke is a very non-manly drink (as is any soft-drink that lacks sugar), and no self-respecting man can sit on his front porch and drink one of these. With the $1 I will get for this, I am going to purchase a 40oz of Old E Ice 800. My wife allows me to drink this beverage on the front porch as long as it is in a paper bag. The Diet Coke was purchased as a 12 pack last weekend for $5. You can get 2/3 of that twelve pack for $1. By using the simple cross-multiply and divide function that you learned in middle school you can easily conclude that 2/3 of $5 is way more than $1. This is by far the best deal you will ever get on Diet Coke. Call or text me at 931-249-7016. I'm still selling off everything in my house and I only have a month to go. If you're looking for more good deals, search "7016" and if you're not busy this weekend, come by my garage sale . . . everything is going for $1: http://clarksville.craigslist.org/gms/3047582557.html

- Location: Clarksville (Sango)
- it's NOT ok to contact this poster with services or other commercial interests

PostingID: 3062854450

This is one of the few items that I ever delivered. The woman who wanted it lived about 30 minutes from me. I was headed in her direction, so she met me near my destination. We completed the sale in a bank parking lot.

Kids Bicycle with Helmet—Dora the Explorer—$10 (Clarksville (Sango))

Date: 2012-06-05, 1:11PM EDT
Reply to: *your anonymous craigslist address will appear here*

I'm selling this rugged Dora the Explorer bicycle with training wheels and a matching Dora the Explorer Helmet for only $10. This bike is top-of-the-line (in my opinion). It has a stiff front suspension and rides low to the ground to help minimize injuries due to falling off the bike. It has a "classy" paint job and is a regular conversation piece throughout the neighborhood among kids 4 and under. The helmet is made of styrofoam and hardened plastic. It looks real nice. If you're interested in paying my firm price of $10, then text or cal me at 931-249-7016.

- Location: Clarksville (Sango)
- it's NOT ok to contact this poster with services or other commercial interests

PostingID: 3058958133

Garage / Moving Sale—July 7, 8am (Clarksville (Sango))

Date: 2012-06-29, 11:58AM EDT
Reply to: kt4xf-3108508894@sale.craigslist.org

Because of my awesomeness, I have sold almost everything in my house on craigslist in less than two months. This will be my last listing. I'll be kicking off the festivities at 8am on Saturday July 7th with a moving sale. I will be selling all of the things I own that I have needed to use until the last minute and a few things that I forgot to sell in our garage sale last month. There will be a lot of good stuff at some really cheap, non-negotiable prices. What I mean by this is that I have already gotten rid of all of the "crap" that you see at a typical garage sale. What I am selling are things that actually serve a purpose . . . . and I will be selling them for very low prices. I am however not desperate for money and being that you are not one of my friends, I feel no need whatsoever to lower the price "just for you." So if you feel that my asking price is too high for the cordless drill set that I'll be selling for $30, then that's fine . . . . just don't plan on me dropping the price for you. Whatever has not sold by 9am will be loaded up into my U-Haul trailer and I will take them with me to give to people I actually care about. So . . . . here are a few of the things that you will see at this fun-filled event: 10' step ladder, a carpet cleaner, a eureka vacuum, some large fans, small kitchen appliances (ie. Crockpot . . .), some luggage, maybe a dining room table, maybe some tools (not sure about that yet) and there will be more things that I find as I continue packing over the next week. At 9am, the garage sale is over and we will be moving into phase II of the morning.

Phase II will consist of me selling my washer and dryer set in a fun little auction style event. It will start at exactly 9am according to the time on my phone. Follow this link if you'd like to find out more. http://clarksville.craigslist.org/app/3019716670.html

My address is 1224 Voyage Court, Adams, TN 37010. During my last garage sale, I had a few angry people complaining about how hard it was to find my house and how I didn't put up enough signs. It is really not hard to find my house at all if you just use a little bit of planning and common sense. So, what I will do once again is not put up a single sign, but rather post a picture of a map to my house in this listing . . . . scroll down and you can see it. I do not live in the town of Adams . . . . I live about 3 miles off exit 11. If your gps system does not find my address, then you need to either update your maps or just go to mapquest.com and type my address in. Doing that will give you detailed directions on how to get to my house.

- Location: Clarksville (Sango)
- it's NOT ok to contact this poster with services or other commercial interests

PostingID: 3108508894

CHAPTER 10

THE LAST PAGE OF MY BOOK

YOUR ITEM WILL SELL

If you do your homework and price your item correctly, it will sell for your asking price. I have found that the keys to being successful on Craigslist are patience, a good description of the item, a little bit of humor, giving out your phone number, and sticking to your firm price. Over a two-month period, I was able to sell everything I wanted to sell, for the price I was asking. Just remember that Craigslist is not a tool to help you get rich, but rather one to help you get some cash while at the same time helping you get rid of items you don't need or for which you don't have space. Unlike eBay, you will have a hard time finding someone who is willing to pay more than an item is worth. Craigslist is not set up for an auction-type sale where idiots happily drive the price up to a value well above what it is worth. So be smart and have fun getting rid of your crap.

ABOUT THE AUTHOR

Caleb was born in 1975 in Moses Lake, Washington. He graduated in the top 10% of the lower one-third of his class in 1998 from Washington State University, with a bachelor's degree in Criminal Justice. After failing to get a job with the Los Angeles Police Department because of an excessive amount of speeding tickets, he enlisted in the Army and eventually became an Aviation Warrant Officer. He is responsible for saving Charlie Macdonald's life (twice) while in combat.

Two days after sending this book to the publisher, he departed Tennessee with his wife and four daughters with virtually no belongings. If his plans work out for him, he will be living happily in a far away land. If those plans don't work out, then he will be living happily but without furniture, looking for a job somewhere in the United States.